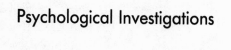

Psychological Investigations

by JOSÉ ORTEGA Y GASSET

SOME LESSONS IN METAPHYSICS
THE ORIGIN OF PHILOSOPHY
THE REVOLT OF THE MASSES
MAN AND PEOPLE
MAN AND CRISIS
WHAT IS PHILOSOPHY?
MEDITATIONS ON QUIXOTE
HISTORY AS A SYSTEM
CONCORD AND LIBERTY
MISSION OF THE UNIVERSITY
THE IDEA OF PRINCIPLE IN LEIBNITZ AND
THE EVOLUTION OF DEDUCTIVE THEORY
AN INTERPRETATION OF UNIVERSAL HISTORY
VELAZQUEZ, GOYA AND THE DEHUMANIZATION
OF ART
PHENOMENOLOGY AND ART
HISTORICAL REASON
PSYCHOLOGICAL INVESTIGATIONS

JOSÉ   ORTEGA   Y   GASSET

PSYCHOLOGICAL
INVESTIGATIONS

TRANSLATED BY JORGE GARCÍA-GÓMEZ

W·W·NORTON & COMPANY
New York   London

Copyright © 1987 by W. W. Norton & Company, Inc.
All rights reserved.
Published simultaneously in Canada
by Penguin Books Canada Ltd.,
2801 John Street, Markham, Ontario L3R 1B4.
Printed in the United States of America.

The text of this book is composed in Janson, with
display type set in Futura. Composition by PennSet, Inc.
Manufacturing by The Murray Printing Company.

First Edition

Library of Congress Cataloging in Publication Data
Ortega y Gasset, José, 1883–1955.
   Psychological investigations.
   Translation of: Investigaciones psicológicas.
   1. Truth. 2. Psychology—Philosophy. I. Title.
B4568.073I5813   1987   121   86-16246

ISBN 0-393-02401-6

W. W. Norton & Company, Inc.
500 Fifth Avenue, New York, N.Y. 10110
W. W. Norton & Company Ltd.
37 Great Russell Street, London WC1B 3NU

1 2 3 4 5 6 7 8 9 0

Contents

6 CONTENTS

Translator's Introduction

Psychological Investigations is an important accomplishment. First of all, the book displays the critical power of a great thinker in one of the most creative periods of his life. Second, these lectures give expression to Ortega y Gasset's encounter with the most far-reaching philosophical and scientific currents of the period, most specifically and decisively with Edmund Husserl's phenomenology. Ortega not only proves himself here to be thoroughly acquainted with the thought of his German counterpart; he also pursues his own phenomenological analysis into unexplored areas of research.

Ortega's subject is whether it is possible to establish psychology as a scientific discipline. That this was an open question may surprise us, unless we recall the historical situation of the sciences, and of psychology in particular, at the beginning of our century. The scientific world was then entering a crisis of growth, which still continues unabated. This meant not only a nearly unparalleled expansion of the various scientific fields by way of the discovery of new facts and relations between facts, but as well a search for ultimate foundations within the various disciplines themselves. We only have to remember, for instance, how David Hilbert and others attempted to overcome the difficulties provoked in mathematical thought by the discovery of new geometries, or how Albert Einstein's theory of relativity proposed the unity of physics when electromagnetism and mechanics were seen as separate systems of phenomena.

Now, this was also true in the case of psychology. Since

its establishment as an empirical area of inquiry during the second half of the nineteenth century, the discipline had luxuriated in factual discovery, but had neglected the questions pertinent to its unity and foundations. This state of affairs furnished Ortega with the point of departure for his own investigations.

What the reader is asked to consider is a common situation. On the one hand, psychology is found to be engaged, like many another science at its inception, in zestful discovery. On the other hand, it remains significantly unconcerned with defining the kind of object it investigates. To be sure, this way of proceeding is not unusual; in fact, it may very well turn out to be the normal way of conducting scientific research. And yet there are critical moments in the history of a science which render this silent arrangement impracticable, or at least highly questionable. During such times, the drive to discover new facts is constrained by the science's lack of a clear sense of aim. A great discovery, such as Einstein's, not only suggests new facts; it also adjusts the aim of every subsequent investigator.

Beyond the shadow of a doubt, the turn of the century saw one of these critical impasses in the new science of psychology. A need for the unification of the field on a sound critical basis was felt by the very practitioners of the discipline, as Ortega himself points out. But the realization of this purpose demanded a clarification of the concept of the mental, at least to a degree consistent with the situation prevailing in psychology at the time. For the kind of object under investigation in this science is precisely the mental, and yet a definition essentially grasping the nature of such an object was nowhere to be found in empirical psychological research.

Not surprisingly, then, we find Ortega considering the possibility of establishing psychology as a science in the context of a definition of the mental, although in doing so, he leaves behind empirical psychology proper for the sake of philosophical or foundational matters. To be sure, Ortega was not alone or without precedent in this venture—we only have to think of Franz Brentano, Wilhelm Dilthey, George H. Mead, and Edmund Husserl, among others—but in any event he is single-mindedly concerned with such questions in this book. As a matter of fact, his approach can be characterized as a methodical attempt to clarify the basic concepts *and* experiences proper to the would-be empirical science of psychology. And yet we would be essentially misled if we took Ortega's book to be just another contribution, however distinguished or accomplished, to the settling of a substantially dated question, or as merely a brilliant episode in the long history of phenomenological analysis.

After seventy years, this work is very much alive and fresh, because the distinction between descriptive and explanatory psychology which it explores is as important today as it was in 1915. We only have to look around to find—for example, in the specters of behaviorism and computer-model and biologistic approaches to the mind—the same basic state of confusion which prevailed at the beginning of the twentieth century about the nature of the mental.

But Ortega's attempt to clarify such matters and to establish the possibility of psychology as a science reaches beyond a merely systematic formulation of the problems and concepts at the root of psychology and the mental life, as he begins to expand not only the scope of application of phenomenology as a method of inquiry, but the very sense of phenomenology as well. A new practice of philosophical discourse continues to take shape in this work. As he began to do in *Meditations on Quixote*, Ortega makes the events of everyday life his subject and invites us to accompany him in *thinking philosophically* the thing, event, or question under scrutiny, no matter what it may be or how alluring other aspects or considerations may appear.

After the collapse of German idealism during the first half of the nineteenth century, the positivism inaugurated by Auguste Comte took hold of the European mind. At the time psychology was initiated as an empirical discipline, positivism had already become the standard approach to scientific research. According to this position, the man of science is entitled to deal with reality only insofar as it is given to him, that is to say, only to the extent that he has or can obtain, directly or by means of experimentation, data of experience. Psychology adopts this approach too—and with a vengeance, for it carries it, so to speak, to the limit.

At first glance, it may seem that each discipline could and should have carried out the positivistic program on a separate basis, since each was to concern itself with a special domain of facts or to come to a sphere of events with a particular point of view and method. It would appear that positivism was a legitimation of the empircal sciences as independent branches of research. In this light, then, we can say that the psychologist, in adopting the positivistic standpoint, had to search for a special access to reality which, although common to all scientists in principle (in that all shared the accent on experience and the given as the point of departure for inquiry), would nevertheless be made his own. This he sought to identify in the manner of givenness proper to mental phenomena, as opposed to physical phenomena, to give it expression in Brentano's terminology. And this proved to be the case, even as he proceeded on that basis without having a prior clear understanding of what his assumptions—and the events and facts that they were meant to represent—could signify. But in so doing, the psychologist not only espoused the positivistic standpoint and point of departure; he also *radicalized* it, for he discovered—whether explicitly or only by way of a working hypothesis embedded in the practice of his own discipline—that he had not merely identified a new area of facts accessible by means of a suitable experience (call it introspection, mental observation, reflection, or otherwise) and the appropriate experimental methodology, but that he had as well found a *privileged* domain of events and relations, namely, mental phenomena.

Now, such facts and occurrences were privileged not because they were to be gathered by way of experience (however proximate or remote), since, after all, that is the proper way for any object or item to come under examination in any science practiced within the positivistic mold. Rather, they were taken to be privileged insofar as mental events and relations, and our manner of experiencing them, showed themselves to be the presuppositions of any other fact and any other form of relevant research. To give an example: if the physicist was concerned, say, with observable motion, then his attention was directed away from himself and his states of mind and toward the facts under investigation, which were external to, or transcended, his own experience of them. This was not a shortcoming of physics or, for that matter, of any other science, insofar as, according to the positivistic program, they were all to be engaged in the pursuit of facts by means of experience; but it was nevertheless an imperfection of positivistic science as a whole, inasmuch as the common denominator of all scientific disciplines, namely, experience as such, or experience understood as an occurrence or performance in the universe, was left out of account or even unexamined. If psychology was indeed to have a proper object of inquiry, then it had to be precisely that which consists of the various ways the human mind has of experiencing things and events, and the new science had—in approaching this neglected but nevertheless presupposed object of inquiry—to do so on the same experiential basis as any other legitimate scientific investigation.

Suppose we grant that this presentation of the situation

confronting the psychologist during the second half of the nineteenth century is substantially correct; moreover, let us accept that the task or main focus of the psychologist was then precisely as I have identified it here. Nevertheless, my characterization of psychology— that is to say, in terms of its goals and procedures—is hardly sufficient or satisfactory, for something important, indeed decisive, has been left out. We must still ask about the *meaning* or *significance* of psychology understood according to the positivistic model. Let us attempt to spell it out as succinctly as possible.

First of all, psychological research, conducted in the positivistic manner, must involve a fundamental appeal to experience. But experience is taken in this context in a very narrow sense, namely, as sense experience and only as sense experience. Doing research in this fashion, however, excludes from the field of scientific consideration anything which we cannot gain access to by means of the senses, or which is, at least in principle, underivable, except by means of conventions or other forms of sleight of hand, from what we gather in sense perception. Accordingly, things like numbers, states of mind, the laws of motion, and so on become idle or unexplainable affairs. Moreover, this introduces a paradox in the very heart of psychology, for if the new science is to meet two requirements at once, namely, to follow the positivistic appeal to experience and to have nevertheless its own sphere of facts and events to study, then it becomes an altogether impossible enterprise.

Let us mark this well. On the one hand, psychology would presumably investigate mental phenomena, i.e., those facts or events which we experience as avenues of access to the facts or events of inner or outer Nature, and which any other science neglects in principle to examine and yet unfailingly presupposes. On the other hand, psychology must carry out this inquiry positivistically, i.e., it must gain access to mental phenomena by way of sense experience. But sense experience discloses only those facts and occurrences which exist or take place in the spatio-temporal world of bodies in interaction, and mental phenomena are not to be encountered in such a sphere. Although expressible in bodily terms and perhaps indissolubly connected with the material world, they are not spatial at all: they do not exhibit any of the traits we normally associate with material objects, such as shape, color, and location. Hence, in one stroke, the positivists assign the study of mental phenomena to psychology, but render it inaccessible, casting it, in Parmenides' words, into that which lies beyond perception. In other words, the positivistic program demands the existence of a science (psychology) which its methodological requirements render impracticable in principle. If this necessary implication was not apparent then, it became all too obvious later in efforts to build a science of the mind behavioristically, or in terms of biologistic or computer-model prejudices.

Second, it is possible to argue that the positivistic program for psychological research was at once the latest formulation and fulfillment of idealism. We may already see this happening with Descartes, the founder of modern philosophy, if only we take a look at the ultimate grounds of his scientific attitude. To put it in Ortega's own words:

Descartes was resolved to bring about a great innovation. Things have only one manner of certain or assured existence, namely, that which they possess when we think of them. Things, then, taken as realities, perish, to be reborn as *cogitationes* [thoughts]. But thoughts are reducible to being states of the subject, of the ego itself, *de moi-même qui ne suis qu'une chose qui pense* [of myself who am but a thinking thing]. [Accordingly,] things do not enter consciousness from without but are [in themselves] the content of consciousness; they are ideas. This new doctrine is called idealism.*

If this characterization is accurate, we may say that one essential dimension of idealism, and thereby of modernity, is precisely that of subjectivism, or the ultimate reduction of reality—in any of its forms—to the status of mental content. Moreover, if the final outcome or development of this position is positivistic psychology, then we can confidently say that the newly established empirical discipline of the mind is as well an implementation of the subjectivistic reduction. Accordingly, reality is to be taken as primordially a state of mind, i.e., as that which we first encounter as a modification of the psyche and, more specifically, given the positivistic conception of experience, as fundamentally sensation. Things, then, so far as this stance goes, are reduced to being "bundles of perceptions," to use David Hume's earlier but blunter formulation.

Were this so, a great number of items of which we are conscious, such as the principles and theorems of mathematics and logic, the laws of Nature, and so on, would become highly paradoxical, if not altogether impossible, since they would not exhibit many of the features which characterize sensation so far as it is a state of mind (for example, as Brentano would have it, temporality and self-awareness), and yet, if at all conceivable, let alone valid, they would have to be either reducible to or derivable from sensation. This would lead us to an impasse, inasmuch as such contents of consciousness, *precisely as given*, are characterized not only by different traits but by opposite ones, namely, intemporality and a validity independent of process, and yet, if we

* José Ortega y Gasset, "Las dos grandes metáforas," *El Espectador*, IV, in *Obras Completas*, Centenary Edition (Madrid: Alianza Editorial/Revista de Occidente, 1983), II, p. 399. Cf. René Descartes, *Meditations on the First Philosophy*, ii.

are consistently to carry out the positivistic program of research in psychology, we would be obliged to account for them—in some way or other—on the basis of the temporal and the changing. Now, these two requirements (to take something as given and to reduce it to sensations) are *prima facie* incompatible, resulting not only in assigning to psychology the role of foundational science, but also in forcing us to discard the facts of consciousness in question as impossible, and with them the whole domain of science proper, including psychology itself, so far as it aspires to something more than fleeting experiences. In short, the psychologistic or positivistic reduction of reality (i.e., of reality as experienced) to mental content and ultimately to sensation is tantamount either to making science impracticable or to declaring it impossible. Following Husserl, we can fully grasp the absurdity of this conclusion once we note that its formulation does away with science as the systematic pursuit of truth, and thereby—and this is the vengeance of positivism—with psychological inquiry as well.*

We can come to appreciate the far-reaching consequences of this turn of events in the history of science, and especially their gravity, if we recast our conclusions in a special way. Suppose we use the term "reason" as the name for that unique power which, in a long-standing tradition, has been defined—in one context or another—as the essential human capacity to grasp the truth. If this is a warranted use of the word, we would then have to say that *it is reason itself which is in a state of crisis*—and with it human life, in terms of Socrates' concern that for man "an unexamined life is not worth living." In this light, it would seem that it is no longer possible to continue to live humanly, i.e., meaningfully. Universal skepticism and relativism appear to have taken hold of the human mind with a scope not encountered before

* Cf. Edmund Husserl, *Logical Investigations*, trans. J. N. Findlay (New York: The Humanities Press, 1970), I, pp. 98–196.

in recorded history, voiding and annihilating reason, inasmuch as its defining *telos*, or goal, is precisely the grasping of the truth. Consequently, only irrational impulses and the sheer conflict of opinion appear to be left, allowing us merely the kind of "settlement" accessible through power confrontation and the exercise of domination, examples of which are plentiful in our times. But, I insist, both this situation and its significance can only be radically understood for what they are precisely as the outcome of the modern conception of consciousness as subjectivistic reason. No wonder a man of the magnitude of Miguel de Unamuno not only acknowledged this, but, having implicitly accepted the proposition that reason is a subjectivistic capacity, also came to pass final judgment on the Western predicament as follows: "Everything which belongs to life is irrational, and everything which belongs to reason is contrary to life, since reason is essentially a skeptical [power]."* In my opinion, there is no sharper way than this to give expression to the origin of the crisis of reason and to its ultimate fruit, i.e., skepticism, or the impossibility of achieving enduring meaning in human life according to the beliefs of the modern West. But, as well, there is no better formula to frame the very task to be faced and the conditions to be met, if we are seriously to deal with the crisis of life and reason in which we find ourselves.

Now then, this is precisely the meaning of the challenge taken up by Ortega. In fact, it may be said that he saw his philosophical quest as the attempt to overcome the crisis of life and reason in which he and his contemporaries found themselves from the very beginning of their careers. Antonio Rodríguez Huéscar has shown that Ortega eventually came to understand that only by means of a new notion of the functioning of reason and of the significance of life could

* M. de Unamuno, *Del sentimiento trágico de la vida*, in *Obras Completas*, ed. M. García Blanco (Madrid: Escelicer, 1967), VII, p. 163.

we possibly hope to resolve such a crisis, and that he moved to elaborate such a notion through a fundamental critique of idealism.

In *Psychological Investigations* in particular, Ortega deals with this crucial scientific impasse by asking whether psychology as a science is possible at all. Thus he attempts to define the object of psychological inquiry (namely, the mental as such). And yet such a venture would have failed at its very inception, had it not been engaged in with full cognizance of its conditions. If anyone was equal to the task involved, it was certainly Ortega, who proceeded with the clarity of mind which permitted him to see that what was ultimately in question was not this or that province of facts or events, or one or another scientific discipline, but the very possibility of science itself and of reason as the organ of truth at its source. Hence, the thread of his argument inexorably led him to take up the fundamental question of truth itself. To this end, he analyzed some of the positions which Greek skepticism had elaborated in this connection. He examined two of Agrippa's tropes not in order to determine the nature of truth, or even to ascertain whether or not there is truth. His concern was at once simpler and more consequential, for he wanted to establish whether the consciousness of truth was possible at all, as a matter logically prior to and rendering possible the nature of truth and the existence of (grasped) truths. In other words, he approached skepticism not as a theory of truth, but as the basic objection to the very possibility of the consciousness of truth and, therefore, of science and reason in general. Only by coming to the question of truth at this level of universality and radicalism could he have expected not only to overcome the crisis of foundations which I have outlined, but as well to formulate a new concept of reason, on the basis of which a new theory of life and experience could be developed at all.

In my opinion, we are now able to do justice to Ortega's

book. In this work, he has chosen one particular avenue of access to the ultimate axioms governing reality and experience, namely, the analysis of the question of the possibility of psychology as a science. For this reason, *Psychological Investigations* is neither a treatise of psychology nor a mere outline of a theory of science in a special area, that of mental phenomena, but a properly philosophical and systematic attempt to examine that which renders the experience of truth in principle possible.

In this light, we may correctly characterize Ortega's accomplishment here as a genuine effort at doing metaphysics. In fact, Aristotle, the founder of such a philosophical discipline, coined for it the simple name of *prote philosophia*, by which he meant that activity and field in which we can theorize about *first* principles and causes. *Psychological Investigations*, if anything, is first philosophy in this sense. But just as Aristotle tried in this manner to establish anew what his predecessors had, in one way or another, inadequately sought, so does Ortega engage in his own venture in full knowledge that it is just a further attempt in the history of attempts to come to terms with truth itself. It would appear that the required enterprise is a never-ending task, and yet one which would necessarily form part of philosophy, so far as this discipline involves the only manner of thinking which demands at once that we ascertain the warrants of its truths and justify or guarantee the very possibility of searching after truth. In other words, this radical discipline of thought is one in which man can engage in hand-to-hand combat with truth itself, an undertaking that, perhaps for essential reasons, can never be discharged completely or adequately. In this connection, Ortega himself refers to Aristotle's wonderfully telling characterization of his predecessors as *philosophantes peri tes aletheias*, a formula ordinarily rendered as "those who have philosophized about truth." Now, such a translation is misleading, for, in fact, the expression is used in Aristotle's "history of thought" to speak not of just anyone who is seriously concerned with truth, but only of those who have sought or seek it in a special manner, namely, as practitioners of the theory of truth. The way of thinking characteristic of such men, as Ortega underscores it in his *Origin of Philosophy*, is "first philosophy" or "philosophy proper." Philosophy is thus seen by him at a radical or foundational level, i.e., as ultimately establishing itself precisely by means of the continual re-enactment of the process of self-surmounting reflection on truth in the context of *aporiaí* (or the consciousness of difficulty or being at a loss). If Aristotle is right in conceiving of first philosophy as *zetouméne episteme*, "the science in search of itself," since it is a way of knowing which "not only *de facto* but also *de jure* must question its own first principles,"* then *Psychological Investigations* is also characterizable as a fruit of *zetouméne episteme*— as the self-conscious effort to continue to explore the possibility of the consciousness of truth and thus of reality itself.

Surprisingly, then, and yet ineluctably, what began as an examination of particular questions concerning a specific sphere of experience (mental facts and events) and as an attempt to justify one special scientific discipline in the conditions of its practice (psychology) eventually becomes a systematic attempt at foundational thought (*prote philosophía*). A sustained phenomenological-scientific approach, as adopted here by Ortega, necessarily gives rise to first philosophy as "the science in search of itself" through the analysis of the area of mental facts and events and the form of inquiry devoted to them. Thereby, clearly and distinctly, the full circle of Western philosophy is traversed down to its origins and is seen to open itself up again toward the future. Ortega has thus placed himself squarely at the source of philo-

---

* Xavier Zubiri, *Cinco lecciones de filosofía* (Madrid: Sociedad de Estudios y Publicaciones, 1963), p. 26.

sophical discourse and has once more made philosophy advance at the ultimate level of reasons.

To conclude, a few words on the translation proper are
in order. It goes without saying that I have tried to be as
faithful to the original as is humanly possible, while re-
specting the requirements of English grammar and usage
and abiding by the standard philosophical and phenomenological terminology in English. Faithfulness has meant an
effort to reproduce the beauty of Orega's expression as well
as the nuances of his argument, and yet the most important
guideline I have followed has been the very goal which
oriented the philosopher himself, namely, truth as such.

Whenever it was strictly necessary, I have either amended
or supplemented the text, but, to my knowledge, I have
never failed to point out such changes or additions: brackets
clearly show the alterations; where they were used by the
editor of the original text, or where the context produces
ambiguities, I have also added some clarification in the notes.
Finally, Ortega often makes allusions without supplying a
complete source, or in some cases any reference at all. I
have tried to remedy that deficiency by providing pertinent
information in the notes.

It would be neither graceful nor just to end these remarks
without making a most important acknowledgment. The
labors and application of my wife, Sara, whose doctoral
work has been in both philosophy and literature and lin-
guistics, are felt very significantly throughout this translation. Not only has she read, criticized, and corrected the
various drafts, both as to language and to concept, but she
has also discovered—by exercising her critical gifts and historical knowledge—more than one omission or absurdity,
the correction of which has improved the result most ad-
mirably. Indeed, I can say, without exaggeration, that the
translation would have included major errors if not for her
help. I would like to add—in all fairness—the usual dis-

claimer, namely, that I am, of course, solely responsible for any shortcomings this English rendition of Ortega's original may be found to possess. Since there is no way to repay my wife for her ever-vigilant and caring effort, the only avenue open to me which may in some degree express my gratitude is to dedicate this translation to her.

Jorge García-Gómez, Ph.D.
Long Island University
Southampton, N.Y.

Editor's Preface[1]

In the first volume of his series entitled *El Espectador* (Madrid, 1916), Ortega included—in the section devoted to philosophy—a few pages that he called "Consciousness, the Object, and Its Three Distances," and subtitled "Fragments of a Lecture." An explanatory note reads as follows: "The lecture, only parts of which are published here, belongs in the course offered at the Center for Historical Studies in the Fall of 1915 and in the period from January through March 1916." In more recent editions of *El Espectador*, I have been able to supply for the reader further information concerning the syllabus followed in the course. According to a printed notice found among Ortega's papers, it comprised the following topics: "Open Lecture Series on Systematic Psychology, Part I: Noology, Ontology, and Semiology, or the Foundations of Psychology. Establishing the Nature of the Mental. A Theory Concerning the Sensuous and Nonsensuous Aspects of Phenomena. A Theoretical Account of Attentional Regions. A Theory of Inner Sense and Introspection." Strictly speaking, the pages published as part of *El Espectador* do not belong in only one of the lectures of the course; rather they consist of two fragments taken from two different lectures, namely, the fifth and the seventh of the series which we are publishing here in its entirety.

Our posthumous first edition of the text follows the manuscript composed by Ortega in preparation for his fifteen-lecture course. The philosopher desired to present in it the results of the "psychological investigations" he had conducted up to that time. In my opinion, therefore, such an expression—which is characteristic of the period—is a suitable title for this work.

The organization of the first lecture, and of the third and following lectures, which I transcribe herein, is faithful to that of the manuscript. The text which I use for the second lecture, however, is to be characterized otherwise. Apparently, Ortega had planned to publish it under the title "On the Definition of Mental Phenomena," for I have discovered the final proofs of the introduction which he composed for this purpose. (Judging by the type face, they were probably to be included in the review *La Lectura*.) I have also found a manuscript which, in all probability, is the continuation of the text in the proofs. Included here are both texts, which I have combined to form the second lecture, since, in my opinion, they constitute the results of a reworking of the original contents of the second lecture, the manuscript version of which has been lost. As the reader will be able to verify for himself, the tenor of the writing is not the same in every lecture. In most of them, the composition achieves precision and is a finished product, but in some the presentation is only by way of summary and sketch.

In our edition, the course is followed by another unpublished text. It seems to belong in the same period, and deals with topics akin to those of the lecture series. Apparently, Ortega planned to have a dictionary of philosophical terms published, to which he would personally contribute. Among his papers, I have found a manuscript dealing with three terms only: "abstraction," "abstract," and "apperception." We find therein allusions to other possible entries, which he seemingly had intended to compose himself.

By way of an appendix, I am also including here two other essays, which have been published before. They are practically unknown although they are of major importance in that they show the connection between Husserl and Ortega. This is of the greatest significance for the study of the latter's thought. One of the essays is entitled "Sensation, Construction, and Intuition," and the other "On the Concept of Sensation." Both of them, given their date of composition (1913) and the topics with which they deal, anticipate in part the major unpublished work contained in this volume and may well serve as a suitable complement to it.[2]

Finally, I wish to point to the well-known fact that Ortega—in the actual delivery of his lecture courses—did not slavishly follow the syllabus he had prepared. Good evidence for this is found in the final versions of *On Galileo* and *Man and People*, which have been published as parts of this collection. Likewise, the contents of the manuscript draft of the course "Systematic Psychology" are quite different from those of the lecture series, as described in the printed notice to which I referred above, since the manuscript draft goes well beyond the thematic headings in the notice.

In my opinion, the exceptional value and importance of *Psychological Investigations* arises from three considerations. First of all, the lectures were composed during a singularly creative and decisive period of Ortega's thought, as we can appreciate by the fact that they are contemporary with the publication of his first and second books, *Meditations on Quixote* (1914) and *Persons, Works, Things* (1916). In the prologue of the latter, Ortega gives expression to an important self-correction. In fact, if my memory serves me well, it is the only one he has ever explicitly advanced. Second, these investigations allow us to participate in the development of his thinking, for they display for us "the intellectual radiance of a thinker as he takes shape, . . . as he engages in the process of fashioning himself," to put it in the words Xavier Zubiri chose to write about his own experience as Ortega's student. And third, they are exceptionally valuable and important by reason of the contents themselves. In these pages, we encounter not only trial formulations of questions along directions later abandoned, but also definitive insights and advances. And this is so whether we look at methodological analyses (say, when Ortega comes to his concept of "nodal problem") or at those presentations which lead him to propose theoretical theses, as, for example, when he mentions the "system of living reason" in the seventh lecture. Indeed, Ortega's reflection moves fatefully under the guidance of the highest subjects. Consequently, the topic anticipated as the theme of "psychological investigations" will lead him— one way or another—to consideration of the great problem of "truth." (I wonder whether there is a greater one.) And he will examine it, time and again, but only at the level of roots or foundations, that is to say, only insofar as the analysis of such a matter would lead him to raise the question of the conditions of truth.

In the final analysis, the theme and goal of the investigations can be summed up by Ortega's own anticipatory formula, already advanced by him at the time he composed these lectures. I mean his goal of "overcoming idealism or subjectivism." By way of the relentless continuity of history, such a task would eventually bring him to give expression to a new horizon of human possibility, to which he himself would contribute a fresh insight, namely, the idea of human life as radical reality.

Paulino Garagorri

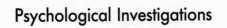
Psychological Investigations

1

Classicism and inquiry. The posing of the question. Nodal problems. Principles and "domestic disturbances." Systematic results in relation to the system previously in force. A general crisis and the arrival of new gods.[1]

As I address you at the inception of this series of courses on Systematic Psychology,[2] I am overcome by a fear the likes of which I have not encountered before in my teaching experience. Up to now, I have attempted to confine myself to the exposition of the thought of a classical thinker. In fact, I limited my work at the university to absorbing and, at most, polishing Kant's system of ideas, wherein are contained—as if in outline and perspective—those of Leibniz, Descartes, Aristotle, and Plato. No one who has ever seriously tried to do this will be unaware that such work demands a great deal of an investigator's most personal powers. Like it or not, anyone who attempts to arrive, say, at an interpretation in depth of Kant's system of ideas will be, soon enough, obliged to spend as much of that imponderable energy we call originality as anyone who would proceed—all by himself and looking at the problems squarely in the eye—along uncharted paths. But even if both kinds of attempt are equivalent in terms of effort, they signify quite different things when viewed in the light of the investigator's sense of his own responsibility.

When we interpret a classical thinker, two distinct kinds of clues guide and stimulate our labors: the objects themselves (with which the system in question deals) and the very words of the classic—words which, as masterly pointers, may straighten out our path in moments of perplexity. On the other hand, when we treat problems independently, we are deprived of the guidance offered by a classic's own words. We then experience the same anxiety that a young man feels when he abandons home and school—those domains self-enclosed and defined in terms of ultimate assumptions—for the sake of the public world, an unlimited environment where anything is possible and everything impossible. Just as we take ourselves to be free from the extreme displeasures and vexations characteristic of social life as long as we live at home, so we believe ourselves immune from great error as long as our labors dwell within the boundaries established by the classic's thought. In it we find a set of well-tested guidelines, which instill a sense of peace in us. The independent investigator, by contrast, ceases to share the burden of his responsibility with the classic as a sort of exceptional witness; now the whole burden falls squarely on his own shoulders.

Against accepted opinion, I would argue that the Middle Ages is, par excellence, the epoch of the classics, i.e., the time when they were acknowledged as classics and accordingly given pride of place within the context of scientific research. Such is the genuine sense of the medieval appeal to authority, which has been so frivolously and uncomprehendingly subjected to the scorn of contemporary confusion. There would have been no need to tell any of the great Schoolmen that the appeal to authority neither added to nor took away from objective truth as much as an iota. Scotus Erigena, the founder of Scholasticism, would have been the first to commend to us his own formula, according to which *auctoritas ex vera ratione processit, ratio vero nequaquam ex auctoritate* [authority has proceeded from true reason, but reason, truly, has by no means proceeded from authority].[3]

We, the subjects, are in search of objective truth; we may acknowledge or deny it, but do not thereby in the least affect its objectivity. There is then a point at which objective truth must also be subjective truth. Here I wish to insist on the nature of genuine and effective subjective intervention, or on the subjective dimension of scientific research, precisely because I regard as the signal mission of our times that of freeing the contents of scientific knowledge from any admixture of subjectivism, a matter to which I shall return. I take this view because I believe we already have ample means to carry out this police action. In this line of thought, Neo-Kantianism becomes an instructive case. With great difficulty, its proponents achieved the level of objectivity, the minimal requirement of scientific endeavor. Not surprisingly, therefore, they felt a sort of holy terror in dealing with the subjective conditions of science, for they undoubtedly feared the possibility of relapsing into that from which they had liberated themselves with such arduous effort. But, in philosophy at least, we have come to a situation characterized by certainty concerning the means at our disposal, a state of affairs which permits us some luxuriance and imposes upon us *suum cuique tribuere* [to each his own] as our first imperative.

Strictly speaking, we do not find in science anything but trans-subjective truths and networks of interdependent truths. But scientific research is not science. Between the two, we could say, is the same distance as between a picture and our perception of it. In the picture, all pigments co-exist in a unity by simultaneity, while our seeing of the picture proceeds successively. We grasp the colored surface bit by bit as we win, inch by inch, the lines of the drawing. Then we still have to put together the parts which were separately apprehended, and we must do so by means of a series of articulations which presuppose subjective acts of comparison, differentiation, explication, and collection. Now, isn't this whole set (the parts, the articulations, the comparisons, and so on) what constitutes our vision of the picture? But doesn't this form a totality with components entirely alien to the picture itself, inasmuch as they are not the elements of it but only ingredients of our vision of it? And even more: who can say that he has seen a picture entire, precisely and just as it is? In all probability, some shade of color, some line, or even some important portions of the picture will have escaped notice. Accordingly, we may unequivocally argue that the distinction between science (the system of truths) and scientific inquiry (the system of subjective acts by which we discover, apprehend, and make such truths our own) is analogous to the difference between what a picture is in itself and the perceptual sweep by which we grasp it.

For my purposes, these remarks will do for the time being. From this standpoint, we may gain a clear sense of my previous assertion that objective truth has a subjective stage, just as a butterfly has a larval stage. Let's note the psychological problem so rich in implications that arises out of this contention: whatever the man of science expounds as the result of his research is presented as true; that is to say, he claims that his findings are not—as are most of men's assertions—mere expressions of his subjective, individual, and inalienable states of mind. Rather he proposes to take his inner subjective conviction as a norm of universal and immutable value. How is this possible? Thoughts aspiring to such exalted dignity cannot be regarded as different from those which just amount to private claims, as long as we judge the case merely on the basis of the conditions prevailing at their genesis. Like any other thoughts, these have co-existed in the inner life of the man of science with feelings and desires, with passions and fancies which he does not even remotely propose as norms for anyone. In fact, quite often he strives rather to conceal such other components at any cost. There is, then, an unusual psychological mechanism by virtue of which consciousness succeeds in overriding the limits imposed by its own individuality and endows some of its contents with trans-subjective value. If proof is needed for the view that we are dealing with a special mechanism, or for the contention that a "scientific assertion" is a distinctive mental phenomenon, we may find it in a curious fact, namely, that certain researchers suffer from a peculiar pathological disturbance, a kind of scientific timidity which prevents them from bringing their labors to the maturity which would permit publication and affirmation of their results as true. It goes without saying, of course, that we also encounter the opposite malady, that of scientific temerity.

Now then, appeals to authority normally play a role in the processes of inquiry. A coincidence between our own private conviction and that of certain exemplary minds is an objective sign of the plausibility and likelihood of such a conviction, the value of such minds being, so to speak, experimentally founded on their secular influence upon countless minds. Accordingly, within the system of scientific methodology, there is a place for *authority*, as a source of necessary, well-founded, and genuinely fruitful procedures.

In every science, the classic figures are those in whose minds inquiry has undergone such an expansion and improvement that we can meaningfully say that research has thereby reached a new developmental phase. Now, anyone wishing to possess fully the tools of a given science and to tackle new problems on his own can do no better than to re-create in his mind the series of profound changes through which the discipline has reached its present state. Accordingly, the classics' example constitutes the foundation for the schooling to which scientists are to submit. And anyone who seriously wants to establish a new science will have to practice the self-denial required in greatly prolonging his schooling or apprenticeship—the time devoted to the study of the classics. The biogenetic principle according to which every individual organism has to go through the same transformational stages that the general evolution of life has undergone ought to regulate scientific labors (although it is seemingly false in biology, as almost everything taught by [Ernst] Haeckel is). The work of a classic is marked by the fact that it never becomes a mere ingredient of the past, but continues to live in what is actual in a given science. Thus we can say that every classic is necessary but, by the same token, that every classic is insufficient.

As a way of expanding knowledge, scientific research obliges us to overcome classicism. The very process of learning carries within itself the requirement that it come to an end and yield to independent creation. Studying or learning from a classic ultimately impels us to emulate what its author did: to surmount the previous classical stance, i.e., to transform, broaden, and renew science itself.

I had to say this for various reasons. On the one hand, as I begin my exposition of the *psychological investigations* I have been conducting for the last few years, I have no choice but to define them as an attempt to overcome the psychological ideas which we may call classical. And since psychology is mainly the work of the nineteenth century, one may better formulate the sense of my endeavor by saying that it is an effort to overcome psychology as a whole in the typical form which it acquired during the nineteenth century. But the excessiveness which unavoidably characterizes my goal should be balanced by the warning that what I am presenting here exhibits only the nature of an investigation: it is a subjective attempt and its appropriate tone lies between those distinguishing respectively the pathological conditions of scientific timidity and of scientific temerity.

In short, my insistence on overcoming the psychological classicism of the nineteenth century does not exclude—quite the contrary, it includes—my profound apprentice's gratitude to such classicism, and above all to Kant, the classic and the teacher par excellence for the nineteenth century.

The subjects to which I am devoting these lectures will force us, of course, up the steepest ascent to be found in philosophy. Semiology (the philosophy of language) and ontology (the theory of the object, the exposition of which is no matter for a few lessons) are studies singularly abstract and technical, unpleasant to the highest degree. For that reason I should have liked to dedicate this lecture to finding a less painful way toward the required steep ascent. But what can I do? Philosophy is an exertion proper to the heights, and, like certain animals, it is to be found only in the land of perpetual snows. In this connection, I am always reminded of an anecdote about Nietzsche. As he sat atop a most high Alpine peak, somewhere in Sils-Maria, a lady tourist who was passing nearby asked him, "What are you doing there, Professor?" To which Nietzsche replied, "Madame, what would you like me to be doing in so high a place? I am out hunting for thoughts."

It is not only courtesy, however, which moves me to write this introduction. The subject to which I am devoting this series of lectures must be justified. Strictly speaking, the first thing a man of science has to establish is the methodological possibility and necessity of the problem he has chosen. I have often said—and I shall not tire of repeating it—that in science the appropriateness of the problems is in a sense more critical than the solutions which may be achieved. The reason is quite simple: when we reach a wrong solution to a well-posed problem, the error can only be partial; at least, science neither comes to a halt as a result nor suffers a setback. But a poorly or wrongly posed problem is the source of comprehensive error, a hindrance and a fatal obstacle to thought. The solution to a pseudo-problem is an absolute error.

But problems are subject, so to speak, to a special regimen. Some intellects well endowed for the task of constructing scientific solutions are nevertheless unfit for scientific work because they lack that most imponderable gift of raising and selecting problems for scientific thought. It may not be redundant to repeat this assertion in our country, where intellectual production may possibly be characterized by such ineptitude. Not everything may become a scientific problem which can be put in the form of a question and even turned into a subject for mental exertion, but often a presumptive scientific inquiry is reducible to just that. And even more: as the adjective suggests, the scientific problem is to be understood in terms of science, for a problem as such is a function of science and, most important, it is what it is in view of the state of the science in question. Accordingly, whimsicality should play, so to speak, an even lesser role in the raising of a problem than in the searching for its solution. For a problem to be scientific, two conditions are to be met: first, the science in question should allow it; second, it should require it.

My purpose is this: to study the fundamental problems of psychology in order to render systematic psychology possible. The problems I refer to as fundamental are not general in kind; on the contrary, they are most concrete. They do not allow for vague treatment; in fact, they demand a most detailed and, if possible, exhaustive inquiry.

This characterization, which is the result of adopting an external approach to the matters at hand, finds its justification in the prevailing condition of science today. Let us take a look at it with this purpose in mind.

The present situation of scientific concerns, a paradoxical one indeed, may be described as follows: on the one hand, one senses a need for systematic treatment and for the abandonment of matters taken in detail and of problems given in isolation; on the other hand, one is wary of generic and vague programs of investigation. The panoramic way of treating questions so typical of nineteenth-century philosophy today seems to run against the grain of scientific inquiry. We could say that we now approach systematic concerns and problems on the basis of the urgent need to treat them with the fullness and wealth of observation which, during the last century, were usually reserved for special questions.

These two requirements are incompatible for all practical purposes. For this reason the most satisfactory books being published today are those which deal with each systematic problem by itself—that is to say, those which treat questions of systematic import one by one and not systematically.

To questions amenable to such apparently self-contradictory treatment I give the name "nodal problems." They are the problems which in themselves seem only questions of detail and yet which, by their solution, automatically illuminate and practically solve a host of other problems. Thus the problem concerning the distinction of the mental and the physical is in a class no different from that of the question of the distinction between color and sound, nor is it any less specific. But once we come to a satisfactory way of effecting the distinction between mental and physical phenomena, we also come to the solution of many other questions, such as those pertaining to the object and method of psychology, the relationship between psychology and logic, the nature of inner perception and of introspection, the possibility or impossibility of a straightforward or descriptive psychology of thinking, the meaning of intuition and thereby the matter of whether nonintuitive thought is possible, and so on and so forth.

Let us now take a somewhat more intimate look at the

present situation of science, as manifested by the nodal problems.

It should surprise no one when I say that the totality of the sciences, the *integrum* of European scientific knowledge, is today undergoing the deepest of crises. Of course "crisis," as I use the term here, conveys nothing pejorative and in no way indicates waning or peril. Quite the contrary: we may suspect that this crisis heralds an unbounded growth and rejuvenation of human thought. On occasion I even think that, quite probably, a change of orientation comparable only to what took place during the Renaissance has already begun to take place in the present state of mind. It is in fact a change which consists precisely in reckoning with and bringing to an end the effectiveness of the principles operative since the Renaissance. And this requires that we leap beyond the boundaries established at that time and advance toward a new epoch and a new cosmos.

It will now be to our advantage to scrutinize at least briefly the strange and variegated character of the present crisis. In prior situations of this kind, a new universal principle made its appearance within the given horizon of ideas, one in the light of which a new world would suddenly emerge. This new world would bring about, to begin with, the annihilation and invalidation of the whole system of truths then in force.

Today's crisis, however, does not present itself to us in this manner. Its ways are more subtle, and it is in fact a situation less amenable to clear definition. The present crisis does not originate in the adoption of a new general standpoint which would invalidate the work already done, but rather—I beg your indulgence for putting it this way—in the occurrence of particular disturbances within the body of each special science.

But what exactly is the nature of these "domestic disturbances," these explosions internal to a given special science?

Imagine the following situation. Suppose that a new phenomenon—not a new idea, mind you, but a new fact—is discovered. Suppose, further, that the discovery is found to be incompatible with (or unacceptable in terms of) certain methods and principles which are at the moment in force in the given science. Now this is continually happening in scientific research, but such occurrences usually affect only some special methods or some matters of detail. When minor principles are invalidated in this fashion, it is feasible to discard them and to replace them by others, which are still within the context defined by the general principles and methods of the science in question. Indeed, such immobility of the basic principles underscores their power even more by showing their capacity to bring under control the new and unruly phenomenon.

But imagine that the situation were otherwise. Suppose that the intruding phenomenon were to compromise the very principles and methods which are essential to the given science. In that case, what would we do? If we were to allow for the existence of the phenomenon, the entire body of the science would be endangered. "But why not do it nevertheless?" you say. Very well, let's go ahead, but not without first remarking on the absurdity of the case proposed, for what we are being asked to do is not simply to replace a principle by a more powerful one, to substitute one theory for another, or to exchange an opinion for a later one. A phenomenon is neither a principle nor a theory; it is not even an opinion. Rather it is an x about which the only thing known, to begin with, is that it is unlike anything else. Even our knowledge of the irreducibility of the phenomenon is rendered possible by the very principles and methods which it succeeds in annihilating. Accordingly, our hesitancy in throwing out the entire body of achieved scientific knowledge is not born, in this case, of a dogmatic stance, or of our obstinacy in holding fast to established traditions. No. We hesitate because if we were to do such a thing, we would be left—at least for the time being—without anything at all.

Consequently, we cannot vacate our principles. And if we cannot, then we are forced to deny the existence of the new and indefeasible phenomenon. But how can this be even a possibility, if the phenomenon in question has arisen in terms of the same laws as the facts acknowledged within the given science? I repeat: what are we to do? Well, what we always ought to, namely, "to take things as they are," as it is wisely put in the popular saying. In other words, we ought to review the principles in the light of the new phenomenon and determine, in so doing, to what extent they could be transformed to allow for the new discovery. We ought then to take advantage of the newly acquired exactitude in our formulation of the problematic nature of the phenomenon in question by utilizing it to settle—once and for all and with the greatest keenness possible—whether the phenomenon exists or not. Thus we would give each term its due, and we would take phenomenon and principle as criteria and measures of one another.

This is what the sciences are presently doing, perhaps only unwittingly. But not only the sciences are behaving in this fashion; so also are art, morality, politics, and religion. In short, cultural life as a whole is following the same course. This is why the most fruitful and serious scientific research of our time is devoted to the examination of what I have called nodal problems.

My purpose, then, is the following: I propose to examine those special problems within the science of psychology which by their resolution would render possible, in my estimation, the present construction of a systematic psychology. And I shall endeavor to do so by dealing with such problems one by one, separately. In trying to accomplish this task I shall prepare for the presentation of each problem by conducting a radical review of those concepts and principles which inquiry would necessarily show to be practically unavoidable. Accordingly, my work will take the form of a series of distinct studies, appearing externally to be independent of one another but being nevertheless intrinsically connected, as we shall have more than one occasion to see. Following the ideal path traced by the object itself, our investigation will seek to obtain results of systematic import. We shall not do what others do, namely, transform a system already in force into an instrumentality of research. (Perhaps later, or on another occasion, I shall return to this matter.)

Let us now conclude our consideration of the notion of nodal problem, the concept of new, problematic phenomena, by giving some examples falling within its scope. We may mention, for instance, the n-dimensional space and [Georg] Cantor's actual infinities in mathematics, [A. A.] Michelson's experiments concerning relativity in physics, [Hans] Driesch's regulation phenomena in biology, and the facts pertaining to nonintuitive or "mere" thought, as understood in the Würzburg school of psychological research.

Here we have been able to detect the concealed ferment and changes which are at work in today's culture, but only within the sphere of science, the region where such phenomena nearly always show themselves most clearly for what they are. And we have merely outlined the most distinctive features which characterize the scientific crisis we are presently undergoing. Since this is a scientific matter, such features may appear to you to be formal and not very instructive. But were we to translate our assertions about the features in question from the language of science into that of art, or morality, or politics, you would see, again and again, the reduplication of manifold aspects of the same conflict. Were we in fact to recognize such a conflict in other provinces of the mind, it would perhaps become more interesting and enlightening, and the look of the near future would promptly become accessible to you with greater clarity.

But we have many things to talk about which are more relevant to our subject. Only to take heed of the great events of the day will I say that they can significantly find a clear explanation once we realize that they have come upon Europe when she is in a state of readiness, that is to say, at that difficult moment when her old principles are no longer in force and the new ones are not yet in her possession. The events have thus been visited on her when she finds herself bereft of inner enlightenment concerning problems of the utmost importance, and when she is not entirely certain about what to believe or disbelieve about them. Some day, perhaps, when serious censure is directed at such events, it will be possible to excuse them by pointing to the fact that Europe was then abandoning her allegiance to her gods and was thereby devoid of gods in whom to believe.

Let me apologize for this aside, no doubt entirely irrelevant or alien to our chosen topic and to the tone and area proper to this lecture course. But, in any case, it has served the incidental purpose of making clear the most philosophical of all principles, namely, that nothing, nothing at all, occurs by chance.

2

On defining a mental phenomenon. Concerning
the reform of science and the change of its
scope. The "philosophical" problem of the
special sciences. The mythological distinction
between the inner and the outer. Phenomenal
being and real being. Mental phenomenon and
physical phenomenon. Color, pain, and self.
Wundt's views. Subjectivism, or the interpolation of the mental realm. Berkeley's opinion.
The stone's being; my perception of the stone;
my own self. Realities and phenomena: subjectivity and objectivity as separable and inseparable.

THE DEFINITION OF PSYCHOLOGY is one of today's most con-
troverted topics, notably within the discipline itself. And it
is today's task, precisely because yesterday it was a neglected
question. The science of a given epoch is an heir more to
the debits than to the credits of an antecedent period.

During the past century, the ship of psychology went
forth equipped with all the pertinent implements—measur-
ing devices of the highest precision, laboratories, professional associations, testing and surveying instruments, learned
journals, and so on. Psychology was not shortchanged in
any way, except that very little heed was paid to the des-
tination of the vessel, however hard to believe this may

43

seem. The research methods and tools of the discipline were devised with the greatest care, but the exact determination of the subject matter of investigation was completely absent. And yet this was the essential and primary task at hand. As a result, we are now witnessing the collapse of nineteenth-century psychology, the shipwreck of a magnificent vessel.

This does not mean that the enormous accumulation of results issuing from a century-long series of efforts has gone to waste. Even if such ventures had served only to demonstrate the error of the old ways of psychology, the attempt would still have to be considered fruitful. Acknowledgment of error is always the simultaneous achievement of positive truth. But, above and beyond this, the psychological researches of the nineteenth century have produced a vast treasury of facts, trials, and approximations which can and ought to be assimilated by one or another of today's sciences. It is quite possible that, among them, psychology proper will be the least capable of incorporating into itself the heritage of the old discipline, if we are to judge by the way it is presently taking shape. Curiously enough, the most influential psychologists are now asserting that forty years ago psychology was primordially flawed, precisely because it was not a psychological science.

Such a quid pro quo can be explained only if we recognize that the successful formulation of the problems of a new science requires someone who, besides being endowed with the special talents required by the new discipline, also displays the keen penetration of a philosopher. It is not accidental or fortuitous that, historically speaking, we always find in philosophy the breeding ground for the emergence of any new science, later to become an independent discipline. The founding of a new scientific discipline demands, to begin with, the exact determination of the boundaries of the area to be investigated. Now then, this presupposes that the new science has been distinguished from neighboring ones, a task requiring a vantage point which does not belong in any of the sciences involved but instead lies outside them. And this is precisely the philosophical standpoint. Once a science has been established (i.e., once its principles have been determined, its methods defined, and its field of action chartered), the specialist may—perhaps without great loss—devote himself to those mental practices arising properly within the given science, without paying attention to philosophical issues. By contrast, when a science is undergoing a radical crisis, and we are attempting to bring about a reform thereof, the nature of the undertaking is clearly philosophical. To do physics, for example, is to work from certain given principles and to avail oneself of certain methods deriving from them; it is, so to speak, to tread on a terrain already leveled off by physics and to move ahead on a surface so secured. But to reform the science of physics is tantamount to invalidating the very principles which define the scope of this science and to imposing a new set of axioms. That is to say, such an attempt would be equivalent to stepping out of physics and resting on neutral ground, at a level deeper than that at which science becomes a specialist's affair. Accordingly, the transformation of physics we associate with Einstein can be seen as the fruit of the intellectual performance of a physicist and a philosopher in one. Indeed, the psychological premises allowing correction of the traditional abstract conceptions of space and time as separate entities can only be identified in the history of philosophy and mathematics, not in the history of physics: for Newton space was an absolute reality in itself, but for Kant it was just a relative component which acquired objective reality only when joined with time and matter.

In the work conducted in psychology during the last twenty years, we can again verify the finding that a reform of science coincides with a renewal of interest in philosophy on the part of the practitioners of the discipline. We may even corroborate the fact by means of a very simple statistical determination, inasmuch as it would be enough, for our purposes, to establish an increase in the number of pages devoted to philosophical matters in the learned psychological journals during this period. In the final analysis, the downfall of the kind of psychological research which began about 1860 is rooted in the fact that it developed during a period of history characterized by the philosophical paralysis of the European scientific spirit; those who brought it into being were not peculiarly well endowed with that keen philosophical penetration to which I referred above. But the reader should understand—and this is most important—that by philosophy I do not mean some vague undertaking concerned with subjects of vital human interest; on the contrary, philosophy is a technical activity characterized by features as distinctive and unmistakable as those of any other discipline. I speak here of the expertise required in rendering concepts precise. It is of course entirely irrelevant whether this expertise is the fruit of inborn gifts or the result of specialized studies solemnly dubbed philosophical.

As is now beginning to be recognized, the radical error of nineteenth-century psychology lies in its very point of departure, namely, in that lack of precision with which it marked out the boundaries of the province of mental phenomena. A deflection, however minor, concerning this matter can only play havoc with the rest of the investigation. What is at first nothing but an equivocation which can apparently be remedied will turn out later to have repercussions which can only produce a ruinous state of confusion.

Hence, defining a mental phenomenon can unhesitatingly be regarded today as the most lively subject of psychological controversy, although just a few years ago it was a matter handled in the most cavalier fashion.

Our well-circumscribed endeavor aims only at clarifying

certain fundamental concepts, reviewing some canonical doctrines, and presenting a preliminary positive formulation, which would be subject to further elaboration in subsequent studies.

After fifty years of psychological research, now that many laboratories and professional associations devoted to psychological studies have been established, and especially as the assertion that psychology is an independent science or that it has achieved its emancipation from philosophy is resounding most emphatically, we are brought to a situation in which the psychologists themselves interrupt their researches and set aside their observational devices and procedures in order to reflect on the nature of the mental. At this point in time they grow concerned with the determination of the subject matter and the problems which are genuinely their own.

Obviously, to inquire about the nature of the problems and, thereby, of the methods proper to a science is tantamount to stepping out of its boundaries: the attempt to establish the nature of mathematics and the mathematical object, for example, cannot be accomplished by the manipulation of numbers, angles, spaces, sets, and the like. But the handling of such objects is characteristic of the mathematician. The nature of mathematics, then, is not a problem for mathematical thought. Hence, we should ask whose business it is to reflect on the nature of mathematics, or of the mental. Expressed more reasonably: when the geometrician is attempting to resolve a geometrical problem, he is standing, so to speak, on geometry itself, or on geometrical terrain strictly speaking; but what does he stand on when he considers the totality of geometry as a problem, and when, taking his discipline as a whole, he wonders about its essence? Or again we may ponder on the point of origin of his inquiry, or on the question of what science this sort of investigation belongs to.

This kind of inquiry cannot possibly be assigned to a special science, for any such discipline by its very nature concerns itself only with its own specific problems. Thus physics does not allow within its scope the consideration of geometry or psychology; nor is physiology competent to do so, for it lacks any instrumentality to handle a task of that sort.

In short, the geometrician or the psychologist would turn philosopher the moment he concerned himself with the general structure of the science he practices. Only for philosophy can geometry, psychology, or philology be constituted as problems. As soon as we realize that every science must, from time to time, turn unto itself and seek to enlarge its scope or correct the general lineaments of its methodology, we shall also realize that the independence of any science is only relative. As is well known, a science's motive for proclaiming its independence of philosophy has deep historical roots and is characteristic of that sovereign mental proclivity which was introduced during the Renaissance and is presently coming to an end. The declaration of independence is, so to speak, the polemical dimension separating the Modern Era from the Middle Ages.

Medieval times were under the aegis of Aristotle; medieval science was what Aristotle deemed to be scientific knowledge. According to Aristotle, science is the causal investigation of phenomena. But is this not also true for us? Here lies the egregious equivocation, the great and vast subject which is the bone of contention dividing the two epochs.

Pierre Duhem, a contemporary French physicist and philosopher, has written a most interesting book in which we can witness the continual struggle that characterized the relations between two different sorts of scientist throughout the Middle Ages. He describes how some men of science, in studying the appearances pertaining to the heavenly bodies, attempted only to establish the order or the set of rules according to which the heavenly bodies occupied their apparent successive positions, and sought to do this on the basis of a given assumption or hypothesis. Like Ptolemy before them, they simply tried to prepare a table which would encompass the motions of the heavenly bodies. They were satisfied, then, with the identification of a regular order in the variability of the phenomena. Repeating a dictum of the Platonic school, they asserted that their only aim was "saving the phenomena." For them, the *cause* of such phenomena was the law according to which motions arise, unfold, and disappear.

But other men of science opposed them from the point of view of Aristotle. According to them, only he who knows the *reason* behind such an order, or the cause of the *appearances*, has genuine knowledge of the heavenly bodies. Science is not the mere determination of the fact that the heavenly bodies move according to this or that law. Genuine scientific cognition is no mere acknowledgment of facts or factuality, but rather knowledge of the *reason* for such facts and factuality. And since every *reason* always implies an "account of itself," the self-sufficient or complete cognitive grasp of anything would amount to the discovery of the ultimate reason thereof. Astronomy, then, is only an incomplete science. To be satisfactorily resolved, its own special problems would have to become the objects of inquiry of another science, characterized by a different procedure, namely, the method of conceptual deduction, as opposed to that of mere observation. The *aitìa*, or cause, is the *arkhé*, the ultimate principle of the universe which is discoverable by pure reasoning.

What we call physics today is an extension of the method established by Descartes and Galileo. And such a method was nothing but the fulfillment and accomplishment of a science limiting its scope to the task of "saving the phenomena." Physics understood in the Aristotelian-Scholastic manner, on the contrary, was the attempt to deal with the questions of Nature by means of a conceptual or philosophical method. Accordingly, physics was then metaphysics.

The spirit of the Modern Era is dead set against the existence of two kinds of solution for the same scientific problem. According to this stance, problems concerning heavenly phenomena cannot be resolved in a way better than or different from the astronomer's own. It is meaningless to say that philosophy can raise—once again and in its own special way—questions pertaining to matters of astronomy. There is no such thing as "philosophical" astronomy.

Here we find the motivation for the just and long-standing distrust which prompts a proclamation of independence for a discipline. And we must find a way to heal this rift between philosophy and scientific knowledge, which opened up again when the Romantic philosophers Schelling and Hegel broke into the sphere of the special sciences by inventing such devices as the "philosophy of Nature" (or metaphysical physics), the "philosophy of history," and so on. There is no such thing as "philosophical" astronomy, if by such a term we understand the attempt to philosophize about the heavenly bodies. But there is indeed a philosophy of astronomy, for astronomy constitutes as much of a problem for philosophy as the heavenly bodies do for astronomy.

This is what the psychologist senses again at the present time, and any man of science will share this feeling when his discipline enters a state of crisis. Every methodological renewal and every regeneration of scientific knowledge is tantamount to the rebirth of science out of philosophy. Science must have recourse to philosophy whenever the general structure of its given practice requires essential modification.

In recent years, I have found in psychological publications a great number of philosophical studies in which the subject matter and methodology of psychology are examined. It is more apparent every day how insufficient have been the results of efforts to establish boundaries delimiting the sphere of the mental.

At first glance, the task of determining the dividing line between the mental and physical realms does not seem to involve any major difficulty. And yet the initial solutions to this problem are in the nature of myths. Our consciousness has a ready supply of mythological accounts with which spontaneously to come to terms with the problems it encounters. A myth is a metaphor oblivious of itself. In the tale of Prometheus' theft of the fire of the gods, for instance, we may find an excellent symbol or metaphor for lightning, but if we were to take it as the formulation of the reality of lightning, the metaphor would instantly become a myth.

Now then, the pair "internal and external" seems to be the most readily available myth by which we can distinguish between the mental and physical spheres. The physical domain would be the external, while the mental would be the internal. And indeed, "external" and "internal" are terms expressing mutual incompatibility and thereby complete difference. But they say more, for they indicate as well that the given opposition is analogous to that between the surface of visible bodies and what lies behind it. And here is the hidden comparison and metaphor. By pointing this out, we make clear how insufficient these terms are to express the distinction between the mental and the physical, since only within the physical realm or in the material object do we find the opposition between internality and externality strictly speaking.

But once we reduce a myth to the status of mere metaphor, we are permitted to utilize it only as a base for the beginnings of an inquiry which will lead us, step by step, toward the exact conception and formulation of the genuine distinction.

In regarding the mental as an internal domain, we succeed only in noting that such a sphere, whatever it may intrinsically be, is other than the external. A separate inquiry will then be needed to determine the nature of the mental.

But it would be useful, before going any further, to establish most clearly the character of the region in which we are moving and the marks distinctive of the area where we must attempt to resolve the problem vexing us. In my opinion, an example borrowed from physics may provide some guidance in our predicament. It has always been true that what we in fact encounter in the experience of motion is obviously different from what we actually find in the experience of heat. Before the time of Julius Robert Meyer, the physicist attempting to explain motion began with the visible phenomena and constructed a theory presupposing the existence of atoms, pure vibratory matter, and so on. Visually accessible motion was thus regarded as the appearance or manifestation of an invisible reality. The same approach was adopted toward the phenomena of heat. But since perceived heat and perceived motion were phenomenally distinct, the latent reality which was assumed in order to explain heat had to be different from that accepted to account for motion. After Meyer's time, however, the situation altogether changed in this regard, as indeed it had to, because Meyer had identified the mechanical equivalent of heat. His determination established that the phenomena in question, although qualitatively different, were nevertheless quantitatively equivalent. In physics, numerical values give expression to those latent realities which are rationally constructed as explanatory hypotheses. Accordingly, in this context, to be and to have a value are synonymous, and equivalence is tantamount to equality of essence. The discovery of the mechanical equivalent of heat implies that heat and motion, however different they may be as immediate appearances, are nevertheless expressions of one and the same physical or corporeal reality. Therefore, the two corresponding branches of physics, formerly regarded as independent of one another, are now to be taken as forming one and the same whole.

This example may help us to understand the fact that there are two regions of reality, or, technically speaking, two areas of objectivity. First of all, we find the domain of appearances, or of things which are immediately present to us. Second, we have those things which become available to us only mediately, i.e., those which are the correlates of thinking or hypothesis-making, although—for reasons this is not the place to examine—such things are in fact regarded as the genuine reality, the reality par excellence.

In view of what will occupy us next, we must now attempt to clarify the distinction between phenomenal and real being. We may formally define phenomenal being as that which is present as such, or, equivalently, as that manner of being which contains in its essence nothing but what is given in immediate presence. Real being, on the other hand, is never immediately present; rather, it is that which is mediated by the phenomenon or the appearance. A real being (e.g., "this table") is thus never immediately given to me. Only a part or a profile of the table is accessible at any one time. The surface of this real table has a reverse side, but now only the top is present to me. The reverse side (and, for that matter, anything else about the table which I do not actually see at the moment) is given to me in a peculiar fashion, namely, by way of the availability of the absent. I *know* that the rest of the table is there, but it is not in fact present to me as such. Above and beyond what I actually see, nothing but *knowledge* about the rest of the table is at my disposal.

Now then, when we ask about the nature of the mental, we are, to begin with, inquiring only into what the mental is *qua* phenomenon, i.e., into the characteristics which it displays insofar as it is immediately present, just as, in their own sphere, heat and motion, or red and blue, exhibit, *qua* mere phenomena, distinctive features which are evident to us and which do not originate in a rational distinction effected by us.

If formulated exactly, our question would run like this: Do mental phenomena, as opposed to physical phenomena, exist? And if they do, and if indeed the two constitute distinct orders of phenomena, which features would establish them as different?

Whatever the answer to our question, we could still be faced with the same situation we encountered in thermodynamics, namely, that although we are dealing with different sorts of phenomena, reason may nevertheless force us to conclude that they are identical realities. But then again the opposite situation could also come to pass, as for example happens in the case of electricity: the latter does not become present to us by displaying phenomenal characteristics of its own, for we do not have a *special* sense to grasp it, and yet, upon reflection, we are inclined to constitute it as a reality *sui generis*. In short: the question as to whether, side by side with the reality "physical energy," there is another called "soul," or whether "soul" is, strictly speaking, another form of "physical energy," is a matter having nothing to do with the problem at hand. Here we are concerned only with the initial problem of psychology, while such difficulties constitute the concluding problem of the discipline.

It is most important to resolve one problem independently of the other, for seemingly there are two sorts of error in science: one pertains to the definition of the problem dealt with in the given field of inquiry, and the other concerns the solution thereof. Of the two the former is the graver, since once we have genuinely formulated a problem, erring in attempting to reolve it can mean only a partial failure, and the scientific work engaged in will not go to waste. But when we insufficiently grasp the nature of a problem, we are necessarily led to a totally useless solution, and then we have to begin anew.

We agreed before that nothing is in fact achieved by merely referring to the physical as the external and to the mental as the internal. The distinction in question, we argued, was based on a myth if we took it seriously, and on an insufficient metaphor if we regarded it for what it truly is. And the reason was that since the term "external" refers only to the visible, the term "internal" can give expression only to the negative component contained in the notion of invisibility. Now then, a phenomenal difference can never be adequately conveyed by means of a negative concept, since a phenomenon is always something positive [*or* of its own], and, accordingly, never the mere negation of another. If, for example, we tell someone who suffers from anopsia (blindness to red) that red is not blue, not yellow, not any other particular color, we may have supplied him with a device for getting along in the world, but red will continue to be unavailable to him. It's worth repeating: we are searching not for conceptual distinctions but for phenomenal differences, and the latter cannot be constructed. We are not after concepts, but in pursuit of names which would render something present in phenomenal immediacy. Only afterward, while holding fast to what is most clearly in our grasp, might we attempt to define or describe it.

We may also understand "externality" as referring to what lies outside our bodies; "internality" would then refer to what lies within our bodies, the intracorporeal. This manner of approach would in fact be helpful in giving expression to the mental sphere, although only to a limited part of it. For instance, a physical pain is in fact something occurring in our body; the body itself is hurting, and, as opposed to the color of the body,[1] such a bodily pain is an intracorporeal phenomenon. In terms of color and shape, my body is no different from the other external things, but, insofar as it hurts, it certainly is.

But while pain seems to belong to the internal domain when contrasted, say, with the color of the body, it appears as external when opposed to certain other phenomena, in reference to which "internal" would acquire a third or additional new sense. Pain is pain only if it belongs to *my* body, and we may therefore ask to what dimension or domain of the phenomenon "being mine" corresponds. The body is not *I*, for it is just mine, but, being other than I, it is nevertheless, and at once, intimately related to me and pertaining to me as my own. A bodily pain is almost always accompanied by a nonbodily component—the displeasure and vexation it occasions in me. The vexation is mine, being in me, and yet it lies more inwardly in *me* than does the body proper. It is I who am vexed, while my body, content in hurting, is not. Feeling, then, is internal, and pain, when contrasted with feeling, is external.

We may pursue even further the analysis of the essential articulations obtaining within the world we are inaccurately referring to as internal, provided of course that our purpose is to mark out and establish its boundaries. Even feeling may come to appear to us as external; the establishment of this conclusion would require only the discovery of areas more intimately my own, or found more inwardly in me. Sadness and joy, for example, are aspects or colorations which I certainly find in me; they undoubtedly are parts of myself, as green is of the emerald. But this already suggests that the ego lies behind such determinations, insofar as they are its colorations. In other words, the ego owns and contains such aspects, which it finds within itself, as before it found pain in the body. It is to be noted that there is a passive relationship between the ego and its sadness, for instance, as if the latter did not originate in the former, and did not form a unity with it. The ego witnesses its passion as one attends a performance, and, consequently, there is a separation and a distance between them. But when I say "I will," my willing is not merely something I find in myself, though it originates in and is born of me. My ego is also actively involved therein; it is as if my willing and my ego were inseparable.

As is evident, this attempt to formulate the content of the dichotomy "external/internal" takes us from one pair of opposites to another, and from that to still another, and so on, ad infinitum, and it thus succeeds only in producing merely relative and contradictory differentiations. Whatever is internal in terms of one such pair becomes external in terms of another.

In the face of such difficulties, what position may we adopt? Since the second half of the nineteenth century, the normal and most generalized reply has been the denial of the existence of any distinction between mental and physical phenomena. But doesn't this contention imply that psychology is not an independent science?

Let us attempt to establish very briefly what [Wilhelm] Wundt thought on this central problem. After all, Wundt, a thinker reaching maturity around 1870, has been a key representative of psychology for thirty years.

According to Wundt, phenomena as such are neither mental nor physical. Every phenomenon (that is, whatever I encounter immediately and before it is subjected to intellectual comparisons and distinctions) exhibits the twofold nature of being subjective and objective. Strictly speaking, we could not even say that much, for subjectivity and objectivity are determinations resulting from an effort at abstraction; they are the fruits of a theoretical endeavor. For Wundt, however, a phenomenon is a way of being which is prior to any distinction; it is immediate being; it is reality given in its originary concreteness and fullness. The so-called physical world is a constructed world, a work resulting from abstraction, a mediated world, while reality is given to us.

I wish to emphasize this point as a conclusion implicit in Wundt's thought. In fact, I take it to be a consequence of his words as inescapable as it is disturbing. According to him, the real is given to us as *our* reality, as forming one indivisible unit with us. And this amounts to saying that it is nothing but immediate experience, or that there is something united with me, in which *I* am just a parenthetical remark and a general dimension. The stone is, first of all, not just a stone, but the stone as it is for me, or the stone *qua* presentation. On this basis, it may be argued that the stone, too, is an object of study for psychology. Now, opinions such as this are becoming compellingly odious to the new researchers in the field. In my judgment, this is a most important development. In fact, such a change foreshadows not only a new time, indeed not even just a new century, but also a new era.

Only in one essential respect does the Renaissance complement the achievements of classical philosophy. We can say that except for those special moments in which Plato, as if standing on summits above history, went beyond his times, Greece was ignorant about just one thing, the idea of the ego. It is a curious fact that even at first blush we find evidence of this absence, inasmuch as the various exponents of classical philosophy do not even use the term, for they do not speak of the ego as we do (i.e., as the subject of consciousness) but refer instead to a social and collective subject. In its place, Plato himself employs the term *hemeis*, the equivalent of "we." But the Renaissance radically transformed our concept of the world, thereby altering the meaning of being itself.

For the Ancients, the reality of being is the most natural thing. They encounter only one serious difficulty about it: they are troubled with finding a way to justify the fact that we think of it, that it becomes subjective. By contrast, those thinkers of the Renaissance whose orientation is consolidated in Descartes move along the opposite path, for they regard being as the product of mediation. The deformation which my thinking may possibly produce in being is found prior to being. Reality is thus the object of their distrust. They are interested in the subject thinking the thing, rather than in the thing thought by it, whatever the direction of their regard may be. Accordingly, for them the most serious difficulty lies in accounting for the fact that thinking (or the subjective dimension) becomes objective, that it succeeds in going beyond itself to coincide with being.

To be sure, the discovery of the ego has enriched scientific knowledge beyond measure. For centuries, subjectivism was the highest theoretical virtue. But as it happens, every virtue turns into its opposite when it is carried to extremes. And subjectivism has undergone precisely this transformation, becoming a vice, nay, a malady. I am now speaking not symbolically but literally. I would like to remind you that the origin of certain mental disorders (*psicosis*)—of certain apraxias and aphasias, of certain forms of stuttering—is to be found in subjectivism, when the latter is individualized and carried to an extreme. I say this only as clarification and not to prove my point, since this is not the place to explain in what sense we can, strictly speaking, talk about socially prevalent maladies of the mind.

Drawing on the results of my prior, provisional analysis, I would then say that by subjectivism I mean the inclination to move back from the relatively external to the relatively internal and, thereby, to interpolate the sphere of the mental between the ego (as engaged in the activity of knowing) and the physical world.

Let us now venture into a new analysis, even if we reduce it to its bare essentials. In my opinion, once [George] Berkeley's thought is corrected, so is Wundt's as well. The moment Wundt's errors are rectified, so too are those committed by [Theodor] Lipps, Wundt's great rival just recently deceased. And rectifying the stances adopted by Wundt and Lipps will also allow us to correct the position taken by [Paul] Natorp, who, as is customary with him, carries this manner of thinking to heroic extremes.

For technical reasons and also purposes of my own, I would like to focus my analysis on Natorp's views. Precisely because I shared them once and they served as a vigorous basis for molding my own system of ideas, I am obliged to explain carefully why I have been led to abandon them almost completely. Now, Natorp's psychology is essentially systematic: he employs his general philosophical system as a means for reaching psychological conceptualizations, which are quite complicated in themselves. Accordingly, I will exclude in this summary any formal reference to Natorp's work, although, in a fuller exposition of it, I will devote an entire chapter to a commentary on his views.[2]

Let us start by inquiring into the grounds upon which Berkeley may contend that any entity whatever is, to begin with, a part of a mind or an ego. The answer is already at hand, since we have just seen that we cannot *think* about anything of which we assert existence or being as if it were unrelated to some ego which would perceive it, or be its witness. Against this contention, no possible objection can be raised, once we realize that the impossibility in question pertains to thought as such, i.e., once we see that what is involved is a rational or conceptual impossibility. But we have already noted that the world *qua* object of thought cannot be identified with phenomenal being, inasmuch as the former is intellectually constructed. We may not be able to think of matter except as composed of atoms or the appropriate substitutes thereof, but we may certainly *see* material objects without the benefit of atoms.

Berkeley's reasoning may be meaningful within the metaphysical order. As a matter of fact, it may very well be true—as [Henri] Bergson argues today, and Berkeley had done before him—that matter is but a form of the mind, or that the *ideal reality* of *physis* is only *psyche*. But even in this context, the reasoning involved may rightfully be turned around. If *A* cannot exist without being perceived or without being in me, my perceiving likewise must needs perceive something, *my* particular *A*. For *A* is not just identical with perceiving. If it were, then perceiving *A* would be the same as perceiving a perceiving, and so on, ad infinitum. (Such infinite regress is the lot to which Berkeley's subjectivism is fated, as is also Fichte's, although Fichte's form of subjectivism seems, at first blush, so different from Berkeley's.) But no such thing is the case. Being perceived by me may very well be one of the conditions which the stone must meet in order to exist (although the sense in which this condition is taken remains to be specified), and yet, on this reckoning, it does not follow that my perceiving of the stone and the stone itself are one and the same. If the stone cannot do without me, it is no less true that I stand in need of the stone.

But this is a fact insofar as I grasp the situation by means of reasoning, or by establishing a relationship between pure concepts—that is to say, by stressing the point that being unable to separate a thing from someone who would perceive it is an incapacity or an impossibility inherent in thought itself. I cannot *think*, for instance, of an actual color which is not extended on *some* surface, no matter how small the latter may be. Color and extension are inseparable both rationally and in that sort of reality I call genuine, i.e., anything which is the correlate of reason. And yet it is a fact that just this minute my consciousness is busy only with the color of this table, that in my present consciousness there is no awareness of extension. In other words, it is quite possible that the only thing now making its appearance before me is a color. (This space as opposed to space as a whole.)

Now then, when I perceive the stone, I do not perceive anything but—or nothing appears (*phaínetai*) before me except—the stone itself. I grasp only the object which is so alien to me—the thing occupying some space over there, some distance away from my body. To be sure, my perceiving is now taking place, it is being enacted (*verificándose*) at the same time that the stone is being perceived by me or is the *terminus*, counterpart, or correlate of my consciousness. And yet *I am not perceiving my perceiving*. My perceiving therefore does not exist for me. When I direct my glance at the stone, I am regarding only the stone; I am not as well, so to speak, looking askance at myself. The thing in question, that which I call a stone and which does not share in anything of mine, makes its appearance just by itself. I find only the stone, and not the stone as enveloped by me.

On the other hand, I can change the focus of my attention, displacing it away from the thing I call a stone and toward that which I may call my perceiving of the stone. When that occurs, my perceiving, and not the stone, is placed before me. It is then that perceiving appears immediately to me as mine and only mine. But we would have to make the same point, *mutatis mutandis*, if, instead of the perceiving, we spoke of a desiring, a willing, or a refusing.

Someone could perhaps argue that, whenever "my" perception of the stone is the object of my grasp, what shows itself before me is not only my perceiving of the stone but the stone as well. But this is a mere grammatical objection. My perceiving of the stone does not share in the stony character of its object, just as in "navy blue" we do not find anything specifically relevant to seafaring. "Stony" in one case, and "navy" in another, are but means of qualifying or modifying a noun. And just as perception is one among many possible specifications of mental act in general (as memory, volition, and doubt also are), perception itself becomes differentiated in terms of color or sound, and the perception of color becomes differentiated in terms of shape (as in the case of the stone), of odor, of particular shades (as navy blue), and so on, down to the lowest level of individuation.

Accordingly, it is evident, first of all, that the fact that subject and object are inseparable insofar as they are real does not imply that they are inseparable and identical *qua* phenomena.

Second, it is evident above all that the mental and the physical are given to us as different kinds of phenomena at the same level of immediacy. It is impossible to reduce one sphere to the other. We can neither reduce the mental to the physical (as the extreme form of sensationalism we find in [Richard] Avenarius, [Ernst] Mach, and [Theodor] Ziehen attempts to do) nor reduce the physical to the mental (as Berkeley's idealism, or Wundt, or Lipps, or Natorp would have it).

Now, the second conclusion is most important, since, in my opinion, it is to become the point of departure adopted by philosophy in the near future and, therefore, the way of regarding the world which will prevail tomorrow.

Doesn't this finding imply countless consequences for us? And doesn't this new attempt to distinguish the two spheres in question cast a new light on the rest of the philosophical enterprise? What sort of new clarity do we achieve by going beyond a differentiation of the spheres by means of the originary myth of breath as psyche, i.e., in terms of the device which has made us grow accustomed to speaking of the "external" and the "internal"?

It is not even remotely possible now to speak to these

questions. Here I have not even intended to arrive at a definition or description of the mental. I only wished to suggest how insufficient traditional formulations are, and to do so with the greatest economy and simplicity at my disposal.

3

Psychology as a science of mental realities. The effort to free ourselves from prejudice. Psychology is an empirical science, but a science nevertheless. Three kinds of laboratory. The relative independence of the sciences. Philosophy as a first and fundamental science. Truth as a concrete problem. The essential characteristics of the first science.

IN JUST A FEW WORDS, it is difficult for us to come clearly to understand the nature of the two sciences I have placed at the foundation of psychology. I mean noology and ontology. And yet such anticipation is hardly required, since, in fact, we are immediately going to cross the boundaries of those sciences and, in a sense, to traverse them inch by inch. Suffice it for us to know at this point that, just as semiology is the science of meaning or of the expression of thought, so are noology and ontology—except here and there— the sciences which deal with thought pure and primordial.[1]

Noology, ontology, and semiology, therefore, are parts not of psychology, but of philosophy. It is to be understood that in this statement "psychology" designates a science we are searching for, one which studies "realities," not one which deals only with "possibility" or "ideal being," as philosophy does. I am not now dogmatically asserting that psychology meets these criteria. Rather let us first see whether or not such a thing is *possible*. And yet, to engage in this task, we must have access to comprehensive philosophical foundations. Any question strictly concerned with determining whether or not something is possible is philosophical in nature, and cannot be resolved except by philosophical means. I would not find it objectionable to define philosophy again as Christian Wolff did in the eighteenth century, as "the science of the possible as such." I have said before that science is vitiated when it comes into the realm of life, and— as the drab enterprise that it is— aspires to live off the golden tree of life, to use the words of Goethe's song! Now I wish to add that philosophy has to leave to other sciences the task of theorizing about reality, while it ascetically withdraws into the confines of the general theory of the possible.

Now then, if by "Nature" we understand the totality of "realities," then the science of psychology we are seeking to establish is—undoubtedly and beyond reservations—a "natural" science. This assertion, however, by no means implies that such realities belong only in a given category, namely, spatiality, the domain of that which consists in occupying space. Perhaps there are other realities—real in the same sense and to the same degree as spatial realities— which occupy no space. I am speaking of "intentional realities," those which would consist in taking cognizance (*sentir*). Over against physics, or the science of extended Nature, psychology would then be the science of "cognizant" Nature, if we take this qualification in a sufficiently wide sense. Alongside physical Nature, then, there would be mental Nature; alongside the study of bodies, there would be the study of minds or, to say it bluntly and without the terminological hypocrisy of the nineteenth century, a science of souls.

Very few things so clearly reveal the inmost historical recesses of the nineteenth-century mind as the terrors experienced—forty or fifty years ago—by scientists whenever they encountered the word "soul." Here we find an exemplary case of the role which passions or emotional attitudes play in theoretical work. As you remember, I spoke of this subject in my first lecture. In fact, it is truly touching to see such men finding no objections to the term, provided it comes in Greek guise. "Psyche" and "psychical" were tame words to them, provoking no horror at all. Friedrich Albert Lange, for one, proudly proclaimed the virtues of a "psychology without a soul"—bereft of soul indeed, but evidently imbued with psyche. Men of science took this victory over a word as if it were a victory over the corresponding reality and the problem contained therein.

Is it not peculiar to discover, in regard to a word, the survival of the primitive magical attitude proper to a taboo? And to find it in the midst of intellectual activities, of scientific performances so developed and so rich in skeptical reserve, in fact characterized by the most strict critical stance? This only proves that the victory of freedom of thought— however important it may be—amounts only to the liberation of science from the most external obstacles and prejudices.

Freedom from the intervention of Church and State— useful for the social development of science—has not affected the internal development of science itself, or influenced the purification and intensification of scientific thinking as such. To become free from certain prejudices which are more intimately linked to the very activity of the intellect is more important for the internal progress of science (as opposed to its mere social advancement) than the attainment of freedom vis-à-vis Church and State. Science must be freed from the prejudices characteristic of the man of science, from the disturbances of intellection pure and simple which are brought about by the political, aesthetic, economic, and other loves and hatreds arising in the life of the scientist. It is now almost fifty years ago that one day, in a desolate place on his way to Vicálvaro, Julián Sanz del Río said sadly to Francisco Giner, then just a young man, "I am but a thinking being." The sadness was proof positive that what he said was incorrect.

To be only a thinking being would undoubtedly be a horrible fate for man. It is equally certain, moreover, that man's own standpoint is not identical with the standpoint of truth, since not everything which might be suitable or convenient to man is necessarily the case. Indeed, certain truths may be downright harmful to him. The fact is that man cannot partake of the truth, except by means of his capacity for theory. Indeed, the greater the theoretical bent of his thought, the more he would partake in it. Moreover, the standpoint of the truth is *species quaedam aeternitatis*, that is to say, corresponding to an eternal view of things, while [a man's] life ideally aims at securing the greatest possible expansion of the compass and range of [the] instant, a moment which swiftly passes, never to return.

But let us come back to our topic. When I proposed to establish "psychology," or the science of souls, side by side with physics, or the science of bodies, I was as well trying to break any possible connection which might exist between the new science and any form of metaphysical psychology. I wanted to promote not the foundation of a meta-physics, but the establishment of a para-physics, another science alongside physics. Accordingly, what I proposed was the creation of a form of investigation based on experience, no more and no less than physics is. Therefore, once and for all, let those fears come to an end which apparently are still provoked in no few people when they encounter the term "soul," that ghost of a word. The soul, or the problem of cognizant reality, is no more mysterious than the body, or the problem of extended reality. But let me add that by the same token it is no less mysterious than the latter. In point of fact, no one knows—not even in the vaguest sense—the nature of this cognizant power. But then, again, does anybody know, even vaguely, the nature of the power of occupying and filling up space, which the physicist identifies as the essential and defining feature of bodies?

In the first lecture, I characterized the *suum cuique tribuere* [to each his own] as the methodological imperative of our times. In a lecture on the role of mathematics in a cultural context, which I delivered at the Ateneo two years ago,[2] I attempted to show how the idea of evolution—so characteristic of the nineteenth century—supplied that epoch with the means to achieve its greatest accomplishments, and yet was as well the limitation and the error of that century. Or to put it in the words of the moralist: "Anyone's virtue is his vice." The idea of evolution serves as a method by which, when we succeed in showing how one thing derives from another, we also reduce the one to the other. As an extreme application of this method, embryology has thus taught us that two things so different from one another as the initial ovum and the adult organism may nevertheless be, strictly speaking, the same thing, even to the point that nothing is found in the latter which was not already in the former. Proving this amounts to interpolating—between any two such objects, so different and, in fact, so remote from each other—a series of new objects, which are the intermediate stages through which the organism would have to pass. The separation between the extreme points of the series (the ovum and the adult, for example) is indeed huge, but any intermediate stage is not so different from them as the extremes are from one another. And as we interpolate further intermediary stages, the observable differences between them become smaller and smaller, and the original chasm thus gradually fills up and becomes a continuous path. Now then, it would be meaningless to criticize such a form of mental comportment, inasmuch as the unifying function is essential to thought. And yet, such a performance does in fact begin

by recognizing the difference and separation existing between the objects in question, and then engages in the effort
of transforming the difference into a complete identity and
unity. Accordingly, an inclination to think in evolutionary
terms may lead us not to heed sufficiently the differences
which obtain between such things, making us gloss over the
discrepancies we come across and to search, with undue
haste, after pseudo-approximations. This propensity, naturally inherent in the employment of an evolutionary approach, is precisely the objectionable bent that we must
strive to correct. And we have to do so by insisting upon
what makes things different from one another, thus rendering it impossible to have them all brought to the same
level. For the purposes of economy and convenience in scientific research, it may very well prove useful to regard two
things which are different as if they were *à peu près* identical,
and yet, as long as their identity is only approximate, we
shall have to deal with them as separate things and by means
of separate methods and concepts.

I say all this so as not to be misunderstood as to the sense
of my constant struggle against the "naturalistic" system of
ideas. I am not motivated in such a polemical encounter by
any mystical or even metaphysical interests. Quite the contrary. In contrasting psychology and physics, I am not seeking a way out of experience. I am doing exactly the opposite,
for, in the name of a more complete fulfillment of the requirements of experience, I seek to avoid any confusion
between these two natural sciences. We are striving to establish psychology as a science that is empirical to the highest degree, but is a psychological discipline nevertheless.
We are not going to renounce one for love of the other. If
I reject the notion of physiological psychology, it is for good
reason. First of all, no such would-be science actually exists.
To be sure, the titles of many books include such an expression. Among them, we have Wundt's own, *Foundations of*

Physiological Psychology [1873]. And yet this work is obviously nothing of the sort. It is rather a mixture of two different things, side by side: psychological studies and physiological researches. Within one and the same investigation, we often find strictly psychological concepts and methods mixed up with physiological concepts and means. Such mixtures, however, do not result in a synthesis, but instead end with a sort of unclear meretricious interconnection. At this point, it may be useful to remind ourselves that Wundt himself does not find acceptable the attempt to define psychology as a physiological science, since, in his view, there are other forms of psychology, such as the nonphysiological discipline he terms "the psychology of nations." Second, even if physiological psychology were possible in principle, it could never replace the science we are after, since such a would-be discipline is possible only on the basis of materialism, which is only a metaphysical hypothesis. I reject it, then, not insofar as it is physiological, but to the extent that it is metaphysical.

The empirical science of psychology we are after will have laboratories at its disposal, but they will be devoted to strictly psychological matters. The laboratories will be supplied with instruments, for how could it be otherwise? But such devices will be utilized in research programs entirely dedicated to psychological questions. This is not the occasion to determine the exact boundary line separating a psychological from a physiological instrument, since we are only anticipating the shape which a psychological-scientific project will adopt, while remaining entirely unconcerned with justifying and implementing such a project. There will also be physiology laboratories, which will function in a fashion completely free of an interest in psychological problems. Moreover, there will be a third sort of laboratory, situated, so to speak, between the other two. Its business will be the study of a perfectly well defined problem which will not be characterized as either physiological or psychological in nature, precisely because it concerns the relations between the psyche and the body. In my opinion, things will begin to clear up the moment we succeed in establishing the demarcations separating these three kinds of laboratory.

And even though I am not required in this context to do so, I will here take the liberty of suggesting to the physiologist that for the sake of the future of his discipline, he should carefully free his laboratory from the influence of instruments, methods, and concepts proper to physics. Physiology has suffered under the same lack of clarity and rigor as psychology. To show that my remarks are not misguided, I need only point to the fact that a physiology laboratory of this kind—one devoted entirely to physiological matters, without any admixture of physics—already exists and is acknowledged as one of the most promising for the near future. I am referring to Pavlov's laboratory in Russia and to the methods which he practices. As [Max] Scheler has indicated, in Pavlov's work we find for the first time physiology pure and simple, since he has radically excluded both the physical and the mental dimensions.

We are therefore in search of the discipline of psychology as a science independent of philosophy. To term a science "independent" is most fashionable today, but the characterization is, nevertheless, exceedingly ambiguous. For what is the meaning of saying that a science is independent? Except for one, all sciences proceed on the basis of presuppositions or assumptions for which they themselves cannot furnish the demonstrations. Such presuppositions are of two sorts. First, every science employs specific propositions which are taken as having been proven or established elsewhere. Second, every science is, itself, a fabric of rational performances (definitions, statements, proofs, deductions, inductions, descriptions, hypotheses, analogies, probabilities, and so on), which are subject to a regimen, standards, and values falling outside its scope of investigation and warrant. Or to say it even more pregnantly: every independent science is a theoretical edifice in which some truths are borrowed from other specific sciences, and in which the possibility and consistent nature of theory in general are also assumed.

Strictly speaking, then, the independent sciences are not genuinely independent. Hence Aristotle, displaying great sensitivity to these matters, speaks not of independent but of particular sciences, *ta en mere legómena*.[3] In other words, there is in fact one and only one science or edifice, its parts intimately interconnected, with some components based on others, while all are supported by those we call foundations. We may accordingly talk about the parts of science—the particular sciences—but never, strictly speaking, about the independent sciences. All truths, whatever they may be, are dependent on one truth at least, namely, that which establishes the conditions *to be fulfilled* by any truth. Only this truth about truth, *only* the theory which serves as the foundation rendering any other theory possible—in a word, only the science of science—may be regarded, *in a certain sense*, as independent. And I introduce this qualification, because even though this fundamental science which has as its business showing the possibility of science, and the general conditions to which science is subject, does not in turn presuppose another discipline, it does nevertheless, in performing such tasks, posit other scientific enterprises or at least the outlines of them.

An essential interdependence obtains, therefore, among all sciences or theories. No discipline is truly or legitimately scientific, except as a member of the universal body of science.

When one speaks of the independent sciences, one means then to say only that, *in fact*, it is possible to study some problems separately from others. Or to put it differently: in point of fact, truths may be discovered independently of one another. Ideally speaking, the physicist can cultivate physics without knowing either logic or biology. Even in his slumber a man can discover truths, and yet this does not mean that there are any slumbering truths. We may discover truths in isolation from one another, but this does not signify that truths exist in isolation. By way of this distinction, a difference I pointed to in the first lecture makes its reappearance, namely, that between science and scientific inquiry, between truth and our search after truth.

I have said that, ideally speaking, a physicist can determine the propositions which are true within his discipline without being acquainted with logic or biology. And I have said this because it is the case, a fact we could immediately corroborate, should the need arise. Moreover, it is important for me to assert this in order to distinguish my position from certain quite confused views which are, generally speaking, propounded by the Neo-Kantians concerning the relationship between the particular sciences and philosophy. In fact, the Neo-Kantians are most eager to extend the formal scope of philosophy, so as to have it encompass the sciences within its own field of jurisdiction. Since science is for them, strictly speaking, only the clear consciousness of rational methodology, and since such a form of consciousness is available, of course, nowhere but in philosophy, one sometimes comes to suspect that, for them, the only scientific dimension discoverable, say, in physics, is the philosophical core it may latently contain.

On the other hand, it would be most harmful to overlook the fact that only ideally is it possible to think of a physicist as being entirely bereft of logical knowledge. Actually, semiology, or general grammar, as much as noology—i.e., the first parts of philosophy itself—ought to be regarded as foundations, rational presuppositions of all the particular sciences and also of the genuine practice of investigation in any discipline. Every man of science ought to consider such studies as constituting the first and most indispensable part of his instrumental education. Language and thought are the media or milieux placed between the objects and ourselves. Such interposed realities can be no obstacle or source of disorientation for us, provided that we come to know well their structure and the regimen to which they are subject.

Accordingly, the particular sciences are, so to speak, floating in the rarefied medium created by the first and fundamental discipline, which is so characterized for the simple reason that it presupposes no other science, while it itself is presupposed by all. And this is so both *de facto* and *de jure*. Traditionally speaking, this first science has been called philosophy, a most beautiful but extremely vague, insufficient, archaic, and dangerous name, which, I respectfully submit, we should perhaps be retiring from use, exactly as we do an old servant who no longer performs his duties well. But just as the subject announced by the word "philosophy" is vague, so is the problem specific and well delimited which is expressed by questions such as these: What is truth? Does it exist? And, if it does, what is it? Let us use the symbol H, if you will, to refer to the set of researches that the resolution of this problem would require. We should not then argue about the question of whether there is such a thing as philosophy, since behavior of that sort would be tantamount to raising the question of whether the sound we hear exists.

Let us simply ask ourselves whether or not there is such a thing as the question [concerning the existence] of truth. In such terms, I believe you can appreciate the odd character of our problem, which is the most solid and indubitable of all. Any other problem—no matter what it is—can at least be a subject for discussion; only the problem in question is capable of eliminating instantly any doubt which could be entertained about it. The specific answer we give to the question of whether there is such a thing as truth matters little, since, whatever the answer, it will amount to the same: truth does exist. If indeed we choose to say that there is no problem concerning truth, we can only mean to assert a truth thereby. But about a particular truth we can always raise the question of whether its truth claim in fact holds. And to answer this question we would, in the last analysis, have to agree about what truth is in general and about the *conditions* thereof.

As you can see, our reasoning here could not be more unassuming or less inventive. In fact, what it brings forth is almost a truism. But I cannot help this. Out of this most unassuming and yet unyielding reasoning arises the whole edifice of the first science, which is the foundation and the support of all others. Perhaps it would be more appealing to find, at the very threshold of science, the expressive visage of mystery, as happens in the case of other products of the human mind. But I shall not allow myself the luxury, not even by vague implication, of deciding which of the two— truism or mystery—can rightly occupy a higher place in the realm of absolute values. I shall limit myself to indicating that science and mysticism are entirely different from one another. And I propose that we now try our hand at science. Mystery, then, becomes our enemy, and, wherever we may find it, we must—most respectfully—crack its head open with the tip of our spear.

We are agreed, then, that the first science is born on the basis of considering a very specific and yet unavoidable problem, that of truth. But this problem exhibits still another characteristic, which consists in defining and imposing the method to be employed in inquiring about it. The problem of truth in general, of theory in general, cannot be examined by any intellectual procedure which may presuppose other truths. It would be the oddest thing in the world to find ourselves considering the question of whether or not there is truth, on the basis of the prior admission of one or another truth as the support of our whole investigation. The method employed by the first and fundamental science must be grounded in no presuppositions. Such a science must proceed exclusively on the basis of itself, a fact which is the only justification for its status as first and fundamental.

Whether or not there is a way to build a science without presuppositions is entirely another matter, which today we leave, so to speak, hanging in mid-air. It is our concern here, however, to leave two things settled most clearly and exactly:

1. If there is a science which has as its business explaining and accounting for the truth of the other sciences—in fact, establishing them as sciences—then it would have to constitute itself on the basis of no presuppositions.

2. If, on the other hand, there is no such science in fact and, further, if no such science is possible at all, then every particular science becomes suspect and can be regarded as one only unwarrantedly and, so to speak, on its word of honor.

As we shall have occasion to appreciate, the fundamental science, that discipline so beautifully but dangerously called philosophy, is not competent to intervene in or to correct or to evaluate the content of the particular sciences. For example, philosophy could never formally amend a physical law. It is not the content, then, of the propositions of the particular sciences which depends on the fundamental science; only the quality characterizing such propositions as true exhibits this dependence. That they are qualified as true, not the fact that they are this or that truth, is what depends on the fundamental science. Only in this special sense are the truths of the particular sciences relative to the truths of philosophy, while the latter—should they exist— would have to be nonrelative and hence absolute.

By identifying this new feature, we have come to gather

all the essential traits which are to be exhibited by a first science:

1. its subject matter is to be the truth,
2. its method is to be without presuppositions, and
3. its truths are to be absolute.

(Perhaps we could avail ourselves of the sphygmograph as a means to appreciate the emotional value of words. Relative or approximate truths concerning the truth should appear more difficult to grasp . . . than absolute truths about the subject of the truth.)

4

Problem and doubt. What is a problem? Differentiated ignorance.

WHAT EXACT MEANING may we assign to the assertion that the fundamental science has to proceed on the basis of no presuppositions? As a matter of fact, we have already answered this question, and yet it may be not unimportant to ensure that what I have said is not interpreted superficially. By the term "presupposition," I understand any proposition the truth of which need not be proven. Rather it is taken as proven, so that we can derive from it the truth of other propositions.

As an example, I may refer to the epistemological theories known as realism and idealism. We cannot accept the reality of anything as being true, since we cannot even assume the existence of truth in general. Why should there be truth? Is it not possible to think of truth as nonexistent? Here you have the point of departure which has always to be adopted in the fundamental science, in the science of the truth, for it has to make its beginning by entertaining the possibility of doubt, of absolute doubt. Only in the struggle with absolute doubt is it possible for absolute truth to find its foundation.

This is the reason why [Johann F.] Herbart used to say that doubting is the beginning of science. By contrast, Socrates says that the primordial science is a matter of knowing that we do not know; it consists in irony. According to Plato, wisdom begins with *thaumázein*, with *wonder*, with divine amazement, with astonishment. In the first book of the Bible, in the opening chapters wherein is summed up the entire wisdom of a passionate race during an impassioned period, the sage who composed it tells us that the first thing he has learned about is the existence of chaos: "In the beginning was chaos."

And I wonder whether doubting, knowing that we do not know, astonishment, and chaos somehow exhibit an affinity, by virtue of which they are all equally capable of occupying this initial place or of serving us as a beginning. Are they different from one another or, rather, are they various aspects and dimensions of the same thing? As it happens, I would add another item to the list of points of departure, for I would say that the first subject for science is the problem itself. Would it not be of some interest to inquire whether or not doubt, irony or self-aware ignorance, wonder, and chaos are, deep down, no more and no less than various manifestations of what I term a "problem"?

In my opinion, analyzing the nature of a problem as such, examining what makes something a problem, is worth our trouble. Even reduced to its bare outlines, such an analysis would prove useful for beginning to deal with some strange objects and distinctions, items which are most unusual in our daily lives but with which we will be much concerned during the first half of this course. Along the way, the open country formed by three provinces, those I have referred to by the useless names of noology, ontology, and semiology, would suddenly and directly emerge, as if seen from the top of a dividing mountain.

What is the meaning of inquiring into the nature of a problem? All I had proposed to tell you in order to answer this question has now completely slipped my mind. It is as if I still see what I meant to say written somewhere, as if I still hear it being vaguely formed in my throat. I now hold on to the word, but I have forgotten what it stands for, i.e., the reality we call a problem. I find myself, then, in the same unhappy situation as anyone among you who does not know at all what a problem is.

And yet I am not concerned. Please mark the following oddity, which is characteristic of any thought. I have just said that I hold on only to the word "problem," but not to the reality we call by that name. In fact, I see it nowhere. I do not even find the slightest trace of it in my consciousness. But if someone were to tell me—let me apologize to you for the bizarre nature of the example—that to be a problem is to be a native of Calatayud, I and those of you who, like me, do not know what a problem is, would nevertheless protest. In other words, despite our ignorance, we would still know that "to be a native of Calatayud" is not what we refer to when we speak of a "problem."

Accordingly, we could say we were in possession of something which is more than a word. Apparently, without our realizing it, the reality itself we call a problem is—we know not how—right under our noses, for it discloses something of itself when we do not mistake something else for it.

5

Conditions to be met by truth. Which reality may become a problem? The centaur. Objects and consciousness. A mutuality of reference. Intuition.

LET US NOT LOSE SIGHT of the path already traversed. We found it necessary to take up again the precise concept of truth and the conditions attendant upon it, so as to come well equipped to the task of dealing with the main questions of the science of psychology, that is to say, with those relating to a specific theory or a special set of truths. Every particular truth contains dimensions pertinent to truth in general, just as every individual body shares with all other bodies something in common, namely, whatever they have which belongs to body as such, *in genere*. Hence, to deal with questions of psychology, we discovered, we had to explain with care the contents of some of the chapters of the first science, the science of truth, on which psychology—like any other science—is formally based.

And yet, if the study of psychology is to make progress, paying heed to the objective requirement by which psychology presupposes logic as a foundation is not enough. Above and beyond it, we must take a look at a subjective reason which becomes necessary for didactic purposes, at one which—following Nietzsche—I would characterize as being "human, all-too-human." I am referring to a common experience found even among the most cultivated people, including those whose degree of development is so high that

they seriously contribute to the advancement of one particular science or another. I mean the fact that they have not
usually found the opportunity to clarify for themselves what
the goddess Truth—to whose service they devote their lives—
may possibly be. It is somewhat absurd to find ourselves
practicing a science, and yet never to have sought after—
let alone to have found—a clear and soundly ascertained
concept of what we are doing. I have in mind the distance—
if any—which separates our possible knowledge of being
from being itself. In other words, I am speaking of our
missing concern for the possible limits which science cannot
surpass in its inquiry into the inner recesses of being. However, perhaps because of that very absurdity, such a situation is "human, all-too-human." Now, whether or not this
state of affairs is as I describe it is not a subject convenient
for discussion. Let everyone's conscience faithfully speak to
him about it, with that clear voice which is born of the
incorruptible depths of his own person.

(In the Middle Ages, those who did not personally seek
after the nature of truth behaved thus simply because they
took it for granted—as an indubitable, self-evident, and obvious presupposition—that truth was what the Councils defined. Similarly, today people fanatically—i.e., un-reason-
ably—believe that truth is what is proclaimed to be so by
the Academies of Natural Science, as has been pointed out
by [Hippolyte A.] Taine, a man so nearly above suspicion.
The subject of our belief has certainly changed, but not the
manner thereof. In one of Pío Baroja's novels—which, typically, is about vagrants and revolutionaries—a character
speaks as follows of someone who is not present: So-and-so
believes in anarchy as someone might in Our Lady of Pilar.
And another replies that there is only one way to believe.
Now, my position here is not that I would be unconcerned
about matters of faith. In fact, in my opinion faith has a
deeper and more enduring role to play than is usually ac-

knowledged today. Rather, what I intend to signify is this: sometimes a scientific tenet becomes an article of faith, by virtue of the way in which people accept it.)

Now, we had come to realize that the science of truth must, first of all, attempt to safeguard the existence of truth against the possibility of absolute doubt. In fact, by making certain distinctions, we had begun the process of readying ourselves to witness that noble step which connects the existence of truth and the impossibility of absolute doubt, and yet we did not harbor the notion that the distinctions already possessed the status of truths. Actually, we were happy to find in them just the means to bring about an incidental anticipation and to establish the habit which would give rise to a more condensed and accurate manner of thinking.

We were engaged in trying to determine the nature of a problem in general. And in preparation, we had wondered about which reality could become a problem.

But let us proceed not extensively, but rather intensively, by studying the matter in depth or by raising ourselves to its level.

It would indeed be a sorry procedure to follow item by item and evaluate one after another, so as to determine which would draw the problematic condition unto itself and bear up under it. Fortunately such a method is not required. In my opinion, the classification of reality into sorts is permitted by the things themselves. We are therefore left with only a few entities or classes, rather than with the inexhaustible and uncontrollable infinity of things. Whatever is the case for a thing of a given kind will also hold for the rest of the same kind.

The first thing we come across, the first thing *quoad nos*, or the *próteron pros hémas*, is what we immediately encounter by means of[1] our spontaneous thought, namely, realities, such as the "rose," which occupy some space and endure for some time. "Real things" we find first and ready at hand, but they do not exhaust the universe or the totality of things. Centaurs and chimeras are also found among things, for we can meaningfully speak, say, of the centaur in almost the same way as about a horse from Jerez. The centaur is the object of my thinking in exactly the same fashion as the hack for hire on which perhaps I rode yesterday. There is only one difference: the centaur does not and cannot gallop in real space. The racetrack along which it runs, and the centaur itself, *are*; they indeed are things, but only imaginary ones. Now then, being imaginary is equivalent to being nothing, if we make the comparison from the point of view of immediate life of which we spoke the other day. As we are used to saying, imaginary being is practically nothing. And yet what is practically nothing may prove to be something after all, if only we speak theoretically. And this is precisely what matters to us now—that things be when regarded theoretically, i.e., that they truly be.[2]

Such imaginary beings as the centaur and the chimera are more than nothing. In fact, each is something which can be perfectly distinguished from other things and which is amenable to clear description. It would be naïve to object, under the guise of great wisdom, that the centaur and the chimera are, *in reality*, nothing but our images or representations. According to this view, the centaur would be no centaur in reality but a mere subjective image, and the chimera, in reality, just a representation. But what do we gain if we heed this prudent counsel? By terms such as "image" and "representation," we are meant to refer only to modalities, states, or situations of our consciousness, by which, in some fashion or other, something is presented or quasi-presented to us. Or to put it differently: an image—which is a mental reality—is an image of something; in it, with it, or by means of it we imagine something. But the thing imagined or represented is not itself an image or a mental reality; as I speak, there are as many images or mental realities as there are people here, and yet every one of them is the image of the very same thing, the centaur. Every person imagines it in his own special way, just as each of us sees this room—which is one and the same—in a different way, corresponding to the particular place we occupy in it. After hearing such a pearl of wisdom, we end up precisely where we were originally, namely, at the knowledge that the centaur is not a real being: the centaur is an imaginary being, a creature of our imagination; the only real thing about it is the image, the portion of our soul by means of which we have imagined it. But far from excluding the centaur from being, this conclusion leads us to place it firmly within its confines, albeit by assigning it to a particular "quarter." The "rose" is real because it occupies real space and real time. But the reality of that portion of space and time and of the rose within it is not and does not mean, to begin with, anything beyond the fact that the rose, characteristically, is immediately accessible in sense perception. The rose is real because it is a visible and tangible being,[3] because it is a perceptible or perceptual being. The centaur, analogously, is an imaginary or phantasy being. Perception and phantasy, then, are but different manners we have of gaining access to being. And just as we cannot conclude from the fact that sounds are not seen or colors not heard that sound and color are not real, so we must now regard perception and phantasy simply as different ways of qualifying or classifying beings or things.

In securing life, so to speak, for the centaur, we have accomplished something else as well, since we have purified our common, living, practical notion of being. In our customary way of thinking, "reality," "thing," and "perceptual being" are synonymous. Moreover, they seem to exhaust the totality of being. Now, having come across an irreal, nonperceptual manner of being, we are required to alter our usual terminology. Let us keep the customary meaning of the word "thing" intact; it is to continue to signify perceptible reality. But we must search after another term which would unequivocally express what real and irreal being have in common. And what they have in common is just this: to be the goal pursued by our consciousness, to be what is present to consciousness in its various modalities, to be what we refer to whenever we engage in seeing, imagining, forming concepts, judging, willing, or feeling. It appears (and we are moving now only in the context of appearances) that I can never find any of my conscious activities simply busy with itself, engaged, say, only in a perceiving, or an imagining, or a judging, or a willing, of an act of feeling. A conscious performance is always occupied also with something other than iself: every seeing is a seeing of something; every imagining imagines something; in every act of judging I judge something and, further, I make a judgment about this or that;[4] my willing is always a willing of something, and so is my refusal. My feeling of pleasure or displeasure flows forth over me, but only so far as it springs from something pleasant or unpleasant. What I have called consciousness seemingly presents itself as a duality, wherever and however I may come across it. I find it constituted by two elements: an act or an attitude of the subject, and that toward which the act directs itself. The act in question may belong to various kinds. It may for instance be a seeing, or an imagining, or a mere act of understanding; it could also be a willing, or even the act of feeling touched or moved. What we identify in every case is one manner or another of being concerned with "something," with that which exhibits the essential characteristic of presenting itself as other than the subject's act. There is nothing so unlike my seeing as what I see, so unlike my hearing as what I hear, so unlike my understanding as what I understand. The lover loves a woman, possibly one whose complexion is dark and who comes from Seville. But his love, his act of loving displays no complexion at all, not even one typically found in Andalusia. It may even happen that the lover is from the Basque country. And what is more: when I speak of something as "unintelligible" or "unthinkable," no one would ever contend that this "something" is in any way similar to my understanding or thinking of it.

To all appearances, consciousness is the strangest thing in the universe, for, judging by its manner of presentation, it seems to be the conjunction, joining, or intimate and perfect bonding of two totally different things: my act of *referring-to* and *that-to-which-I-am-referring*. But mark well the importance of this junction: it is not as if we were to recognize or discover a posteriori the existence of an absolute difference between the two; rather the very fact of my being conscious consists in my finding before myself something different from me and other than I, such as a table. To be sure, my consciousness is not this table; my consciousness now consists in "having the table before me." Accordingly, my consciousness is the indivisible unity of two elements which are as absolutely different from one another as are "being before me" on the one hand, and a table on the other.

First of all, we are to consider the various conscious acts (such as seeing, hearing, thinking, empty or mere intending, judging, willing, and feeling) only insofar as they have something in common, namely, that basic feature by which the acts refer to what always lies beyond themselves. Second, concerning all things which qualify as termini of conscious reference, we are to concern ourselves only with that function—identically found in each and every one of them—of being the other side of, or what lies beyond, the subject's act, of being that which confronts and opposes it. In fact, such is the minimal makeup of anything whatever, for, seemingly, it is necessary that things [actually] perform such a role, or that at least they may do so. Let us characterize something, insofar as it discharges that function, as that which is "in contraposition" with me, or as that which is set opposite me and my own mental performance. In Latin, the word for "counterposing" or "setting opposite" is *objicere*, the verbal-noun derivative of which is *objectum*. In this light, we may now reformulate our simple but important terminological distinction by saying that an object is anything to which we may refer in one way or another. Or reciprocally stated: consciousness is the act of referring to an object.

Having gone this far, I believe a word of caution is in order. In our analysis, we have not even remotely moved in the direction of determining the mechanism inherent in consciousness. We have not attempted to explain anything whatever about consciousness. *To the contrary*, we have limited ourselves to describing "what" we call consciousness, so far as it seems, appears, or presents itself to us. Perhaps later the singular importance of this simple notion will become manifest, although admittedly we have not yet provided any grounds to justify its soundness. For the moment, let it be clearly understood that we have done no more than we would have done if someone who had never seen a giraffe asked us what a giraffe is. We would have described it, so far as we knew it from our visual experience. And in doing so, we would have achieved nothing but the translation of visual-perceptive acts and materials into words or signifying acts. The only difference is that, while the giraffe was available to our visual experience or perception of colors and shapes, consciousness can only present itself to us by means of a "seeing" act which is *sui generis*, since it does not disclose to us any colors of shapes. Possibly at some point we shall have to refer to such an act as an "intuition." But this word is so dangerous that perhaps it should be avoided altogether at present. The employment of this term may backfire on us, as it actually has from time to time throughout European history. That happened first at Plotinus' hands long ago in

Alexandria, whence arose the mystagogic confusion characteristic of the late decadence of the Ancient World. At the beginning of the nineteenth century, it was Fichte's and Schelling's turn to commit this imprudent and reckless deed, for they spoke of *intellektuelle Anschauung* [intellectual intuition] and thus gave rise to Romantic dazzlement. Finally, just twenty years ago, it was Bergson's opportunity to act in that fashion in Paris. The consequences, however, were less disastrous, since Bergson was not paid as much attention as Fichte or Schelling or even the venerable Plotinus, who was the prolific heir to the divine Plato.

(Ideal objects and impossible objects. [This is the place for] a summary of lecture 4.)

Structural Objects[5]

None of the objects we have spoken of can be characterized as problematic. To be sure, the problematic objects do not exhaust the universe of objects. The other day we encountered a new class of objects which seem to exhibit a greater affinity for such a characterization. I mean, for example, the being-white of a rose. We called them structures, or structural objects, since we recognized in them the characteristic of containing—as the whole contains the parts— at least two objects of the first kind. We could also have called them total objects, for they present themselves as units consisting of distinct parts. Someone could argue that the rose has parts too, and that, accordingly, we could also characterize it as a total object. No doubt the rose has parts of its own, but when we name or see it, we do not name or see anything but a simple unit. The parts of the rose do not function therein as distinct objects given to us separately. Perception is a form of simple consciousness. Or to put it differently: the object given in perception always presents itself as one object, i.e., as devoid of any internal discrimination. Perception involves a simple positing, or an uncompound thesis; it is a simply positing or thetic act. Perceptual consciousness is like a single mental ray focused ultimately on the perceptual object. Of course, I can perform, if I please, other acts by which I can dismember the perceptual object, distinguish component objects therein, relate one such object to another, and so on, but this would no longer be perceptual experience, but the analysis thereof.

By contrast, structural objects display their nature as "higher-order objects" or "complex entities," by virtue of the fact that they are founded in simple objects. They always presuppose the existence of at least two lower-order objects, say A and B. A collection is the best possible example of this. Here I do not refer to A simply, as I do in perception, for the connection between A and my ego is not direct. I refer to A only to the extent that I refer A to B, and vice versa. Accordingly, there is a double reference in the case of a collection, for each referring encompasses the other. I do not find myself related to either A or B alone, but only to A so far as it refers to B or is in B, and vice versa. The positing of A, or the existence of A for me, lies in its being com-posited with B or in its co-existence with B. The structural object is, therefore, the specific correlate of a com-positing or syn-thetical consciousness.

At the proper time, we shall see how acts of thinking, strictly speaking, are, as opposed to perceiving and imagining, *synthetical* [in nature].[6] In passing, let me point out that the activity of synthesis now has for me a sense entirely different from the meaning it had for Kant.

In this light, I could say that a subset of the class of higher-order, or structural, objects consists of those items for which the expression involves the word "being" (e.g., "a rose's being-white" or "being A-B"). Let us not go in great detail into the question of why the object "being A-B" is different from objects like "B-being-a-part-of-A." As I have already pointed out, it was enough for our purposes to be able to identify a clear and unequivocal indication which we could use at any time as a marker. And such is no other than this: neither A nor "being A-B" has a contrary.

For those of you who have perhaps dealt from a formal-logical point of view with these problems (in fact, the most current and significant ones in philosophy today), I will only say at this point that the characterization I have made of certain objects (e.g., "being A-B") as a separate subset is a novelty in ontology. In the entire philosophical literature, I believe, one can find a few suggestions which may serve as motives for effecting this distinction in only two works: [Alexius] Meinong's book *Über Annahmen* (1902) and [Adolf] Reinach's article "Zur Theorie des negativen Urteils" (*Münchener Abh.*, 1911).

(A last attempt to extend the scope of the classification of objects: "values." Simple and structural values. Valuation and disvaluation. Simple valuation: the "good." Synthetical valuation: the "best" and the act of preference. The "useful" and the act of "utilization" or "taking advantage." Collective love, e.g., ethnic love. Announcing a science of ethics understood as an axiological or valuative discipline, independent of logical regulation.)

6

Seeking a place for the object we call "being a problem." Incomplete expressions. Structural objects. The objects and the ego: an examination of the relations between them. "Being" as posited by the ego. Two different ways of understanding the problem of the relation between thinking and being: the Ancient World's resolution of the questions versus the Modern Age's. Gods in reciprocity.

NO SIMPLE OR LOWER-ORDER OBJECT (e.g., a rose, a centaur, or a triangle) contains any gap where the feature we call "being a problem" could fit. Such objects exclude a characteristic of that sort, as we can see if we mentally attempt to have them try it for size. It is as if they were hermetically sealed against being described in that fashion. It seems to me, then, that this is the right occasion to secure the proper lodgings for an object of this kind, to search with care after a suitable place for it. And I seek to discover it in the context established by the classification or division we have already developed. I do not claim that the scheme in question is the complete or the last word on the subject. I only propose it as a means by which to understand one another. Now, the matter at hand is beyond doubt if we judge it by the phrase "being a problem," which presents itself as an incomplete or lame expression. Expressions of this sort constitute an important and complex area of semiology, or general grammar. To all appearances, there are certain expressions, for the understanding or comprehension of which we only require the elements already present as components thereof. "Star" or "flower," for example, are meanings we understand without recourse to other meanings. The *things* signified by them certainly require other things which complement them, if indeed they are to exist and even if they are to be seen by us. The star needs the vault of the heavens; the flower must have its stem or, at least, an environment to blossom in, even if it is just air (as happens with some of the diatoms) or water (as is the case with the gulfweed). Taken as real things, then, the star and the flower are not independent of other things, but the meanings corresponding to them seem to be independent. They possess in themselves all that is required for us to understand them. Aristotle called them categorematic meanings, but Anton Marty, a recent author to whom general grammar is greatly indebted, uses a better name—self-semantic meanings. Accordingly, they are taken to be "self-signifying," that is to say, to signify what they do by virtue of themselves alone.

Over against these, we find expressions such as "and," "of," "or," and "but." Each of these possesses a signification which cannot be understood by itself. If I wish to understand the meaning "and," I must have recourse to two other meanings. Taken in isolation, "and" is devoid of sense; the signification of "and" itself is that of the conjunction or collection of two other items, and yet the two items in question are, strictly speaking, neither actually signified by nor referred to in "and." I cannot understand "and" except together with A and B, or other similar meanings. The same is true about the disjunctive expression "or." Such meanings depend on others, and they can accordingly be characterized as nonindependent meanings, which attain their signification in conjunction with others, or as embedded in a significative whole or totality of which they are parts. Aristotle (or, to be more exact, the Aristotelians) called them syn-categorematic meanings, and Anton Marty, again more successfully, labeled them synsemantic—that is to say, co-significant—meanings. Consequently, when we take a synsemantic expression by itself, we face what always occurs when we take in isolation something which essentially is a part of a whole. Consider, for instance, anything that we may describe as a portion or chunk of a physical whole, or again what we call a member or part of an organic totality. The act by which we separate items which essentially belong together amounts to pulling apart and breaking up something. What is left exhibits a wound, a scar, or a splinter, by which we would gather that it is essentially incomplete even if we did not know that it once existed as part of a whole. In this fashion, we recognize something in the countryside as a ruin without having had to be acquainted beforehand with the blueprint of the original building. The conformation or shape of the object presents itself as broken off, as lacking something belonging to a whole, which was once intact and was then torn asunder. By way of privation or lack, the entire building ideally survives in the ruins; it remains therein as an allusion and, so to speak, as a reminiscence. The phenomenological ground for the melancholy aspect characteristic of ruins is found in the way the part looks back to the whole or pines after it, or in the fact that what is broken up preserves the wound and perpetuates its regret over a previous state of health and integrity.

But let us set aside such dirgelike tones, or we shall be led astray. Let us then return to the road we were following.

Synsemantic expressions, such as "and," "of," "or," and "but," are insufficient or incomplete. "Being a problem" is an expression of this kind. "Being A," "being B," and other meanings of this sort signify attributes, and attributes inherently and permanently point to something other than themselves, namely, that of which they can be predicated.

"Being *A*," "being *B*," and "being a problem" are incomplete meanings which are to be brought to completion in this fashion: "*C*-being *A*," "*C*-being *B*," and "something-being a problem."

For today this lesson in semiology will suffice. By means of it, we have gathered the evidence necessary to show that the object "being a problem" belongs in the class of structural objects. This is the place we were seeking for it. For the time being, let us not expound any further the doctrine concerning semantic and synsemantic locutions, especially the part which deals with attributes and which may have sounded quite odd to some of the linguists present here. In fact, my contentions in that regard indicate a position which is fairly unorthodox, if judged within the scope of established opinion.

Now, it is obvious that the fact that simple objects exclude the characteristic "being a problem" is just one among many of the attractions and repulsions brought about or undergone by objects among themselves.

Mythologically speaking, we could refer to such occurrences as the various loves and hatreds between objects, or as the tolerance or intolerance they show one another. Or to put it otherwise, in a way not so rich in mythology although not entirely devoid of it: such are the relations of identity and difference existing between objects—the equality and inequality, or the correlations and irrelations, obtaining between them. To be sure, an inquiry into these matters would result from the fact that *we* think them. Objects acquire new characteristics when we compare, identify, distinguish, or otherwise relate them. Let us consider a particular example. This cabinet is itself yellow, and so is that one too. The moment we realize, however, that both are yellow, a new characteristic arises in them which neither one seemed to possess before, when they were regarded separately. Now it happens not just that each is yellow, but that they are both so as well. The two patches of color have thus come to exhibit a new feature, their equality. And this is a characteristic which each patch comes to have only when, so to speak, the two transcend their respective states of isolation and insularity in order to co-exist. Such patches may be yellow separately, but they can be equal (or both yellow) only in relation to one another. Equality is then relative: it results from the relationship which obtains between the patches or objects. But the relationship in question is my subjective accomplishment, for I am the one who has brought the objects to relate to one another.

I am not sure whether you fully appreciate the resulting paradox. Objects are not equal to each other except insofar as I relate them to one another. It appears, then, that their equality depends on me; in fact, the objects would never acquire such a feature except through my intervention. And yet the effect of my intervention (namely, the equality between the objects) belongs to them and obtains between them. It is therefore as much an objective determination as the fact that they are yellow, a trait entirely bereft of traces originating in my subjective participation. The equality of color obtaining between the two patches, which at first seemed to depend on me, is also alien to and independent of me. I am not the one who appears to exhibit such a characteristic; only the objects do so.

We are concerned here with mastering the nature of a special sort of characteristic, a few examples of which are equality, identity, difference, largeness, smallness, and the like. And we are attempting to come to terms with them precisely because they have a curious status indeed, since they proceed from the objects to us and vice versa, without ever seemingly permitting us to come to a final determination as to their objective or subjective origins.

Our predicament would not be so serious if our difficulties did not extend any further, if these relative and newly arising qualities were the only ones allowing for such an in-determination as to subjective or objective origins, as to their being derived from thought or from things. But relative and inherent qualities behave analogously: like the equality obtaining between the two cabinets in that both are yellow, the very quality yellow of each cabinet itself appears to depend on me and at the same time belong to the cabinet. For, undoubtedly, were I to close my eyes, the yellow object would disappear, and were I to reopen them, it would reappear. And it is even more certain that were I no longer to focus my eyes on a given thing, but instead to turn them away onto another, the former thing would vanish into nothingness as a result; "yellow" and the yellow object would be no more. Accordingly, not only would the object's inherent qualities (e.g., yellow) depend on me, but so would the object itself to which the qualities belong. Now, this is likewise true of any quality and of any object. The entire universe seems to be born and to die upon hearing the voice of my ego or subjectivity, which, like the voice of God, evidently possesses the boundless power to create and annihilate.

But what about being itself? Some would say that the word "being" has only one meaning, namely, "something standing before me." Take one example. When I say of snow that it is white, the term "is" can only signify one thing: that I find whiteness in the snow. But when I assert of it simply that it *is*, I cannot be saying anything except that I notice the snow, that it is before me, or that it is before some other consciousness like mine. Following this line of thought, we could legitimately wonder about the sense which could clearly be assigned to the word "being" when used about something never present before any consciousness whatever. We would have to reply that the thing in question, if such were possible, is not like anything we are familiar with. In other words, we would say that it is neither "this" nor "that," nor anything else, for that matter. Accordingly, we could say of it only that it "is not." Hence, being itself, or that general quality which encompasses anything and everything, turns out to be a relative characteristic too. Being is being *for* consciousness, for the ego. It is the result of the ego's activity, or it is something posited by the ego, just as the equality between the two cabinets appeared to be.

In the Ancient World, men naïvely proceeded on the basis of the view that things are just there, existing by themselves, supporting one another, and rendering each other possible. They were regarded as constituting the universe, as forming together the totality of reality, or *omnitudo realitatis*. For the Ancients, the universe was a being serving as the point of departure and return for everything, since everything—so far as it existed—was in the universe and derived therefrom. The universe, then, was the *ens realissimum* [the most real entity] or God himself. Being signified "standing or being located out there," and "out there" meant the vast domain of the cosmos, otherwise known as Nature. The subject was merely a small portion of the universe, and his consciousness was simply the tiny mirror in which the other parts of Nature were reflected or copied. Thinking, then, had only one role to play: finding things which were already there, or stumbling upon them. Now, this is the humblest position conceivable for the ego. In fact, the Ancients never spoke of the ego as such. Plato, for one, never uses the word "ego," but only employs the expression *hemeis*, or "we." Beyond the subject, then, was the universe, Nature, or God. If indeed the subject wanted to endow his life with meaning, he had no choice but to search after it in the whole, inasmuch as he was a part of the whole. He had to traverse the countless paths of the universe; he had to grope through it by means of the blind man's or the beggar's uncertain and imploring hand. Or to put it in the words of Aristotle himself: *he psykhé esti os kheír*, "the soul is like a hand."[1] Consequently, becoming adapted to the will or the law governing Nature became the moral ideal, the ideal of human conduct. The Stoics accordingly believed that the moral norm required us to live in conformity with Nature, or to aspire to be patient and indifferent like Nature herself. And the Stoics were the last fruit of the mature phase of the Ancient World, living precisely at the time when its decadence was setting in.

But this way of interpreting being as an independent and self-supporting reality could not endure for long. Presiding over the Platonic Academy of the Medicis during the Renaissance, Cardinal Cusanus begins to try out transcendental-word games which, in his own work, will end up becoming serious and far-reaching theoretical formulations. In his opinion, the being of things is only what they exactly, determinately, and precisely are. They are what they are in measure or *mensura*. He even says: *Nihil certum est in nostra scientia nisi nostra mathematica* [in scientific knowledge there is nothing more certain than mathematics]. Now, *mensura* is the work and performance of *mens* [mind], and *mens* is *me ipsum*, or I myself. Here we recognize the only-begotten son of the new age. Soon these origins of a new style of thinking will achieve full maturity.

Growing out of the Renaissance, the Modern Era has been—especially and above all—an age of suspicion. It adopted distrust or suspicion as its own radical attitude in life. In fact, Descartes's genius found in distrust or suspicion the *point d'appui* where Archimedes had sought to place his lever and overturn the world. Things, and the universe or aggregate they form, seem to be actually out there, but we may wonder whether they are there certainly and for sure. Whatever is appears actually to be, and yet, is that the case beyond the shadow of a doubt? The effectiveness of this question endures forever, since whenever it is raised, the result is the same: "being" is transformed into a suspect quality, and the universe or totality of what is becomes enfolded in suspicion. Compared with Descartes, the Ancients were less suspicious and were endowed with a greater measure of naïveté. A thing they regarded as being would be taken by Descartes as something that merely seemed to be. Now, Descartes does not say that something I actually see does not exist at all. On the contrary, he asserts that in fact it seems to be. And yet this is enough to displace the center of gravity of reality. As a result, an entire new system of ideas is born at this point, the system which I have just summarized, and the naïve opinion of the Ancients is abandoned. Being cannot amount to the fact that each thing rests in itself and all things abide in the universe, since we may come to doubt being and may even be forced to do so. Moreover, if someone were able to dispel my doubts, he would only have managed to make me believe that things are what they are. Consequently, being would have become the correlate of a conviction, the object of an opinion. It would then no longer signify that each thing rests in itself, for now it would be the terminus of an act of thinking, the counterpart of the event of appearing. That things are is then a questionable fact, but that, to me, they seem to be is beyond question. My thinking of things as being, my *cogitatio*, certainly *is*; in fact, it is without question. *Ma pensée* [my thinking], or *moi-même qui ne suis qu'une chose qui pense* [myself who am but a thinking thing],[2] constitutes the first and exemplary reality, on the basis of which any other reality lives and breathes. I encounter each and every thing only by means of my thinking, i.e., I meet them only insofar as they are thought by me. If indeed "being" means "being located out there," then "out there" signifies the area occupied by my thought, by my thinking ego. All things exist and are found in myself, precisely as contents of my thought, or as small fragments of my ego.

It would seem that no greater transformation of man's universal perspective could be expected. It is difficult to conceive of a change in standpoint as complete as the one we witness here. Before [the Modern Age], thought was regarded as the copy, reflection, or mirror of being. It was considered a sort of secondary or substitute being. In other words, it was taken to be that virtual existence enjoyed by objects in the imaginary space of a looking glass. (Aristotle himself puts it thus: *deútera ousía, he katá ton lógon ousía* [secondary substance is substance in thought, formula, or definition].)[3] In the Modern Age, however, my own thinking becomes the primordial form of being. But this is as it should be, for, at this point, "being" means "being for certain," and only my own thinking is certain. By contrast, the being of things is merely a virtuality; it is how they seem to be when I think of them.

As in the *Arabian Nights*, the psyche, ego, or consciousness (i.e., the blind man's imploring hand) has become the center of the universe. Idealism, or subjectivism, is the radical way of facing life which prevails in the Modern Age. All the European peoples that have achieved a measure of success during these centuries have contributed to the development of that position. Only Spain has not taken part in the process; in fact, the decadence and waning of Spanish life which is observable during this epoch is precisely the other side of the coin. And this is so because the "epoch," as I understand it here, is an ideal climate, a set of basic principles constituting the moral environment characteristic of a historical period. Accordingly, whoever lacks an affinity for such principles, or is resolutely hostile to them, can only perish or deteriorate, as would the vegetation of the valleys when transplanted to the mountaintops.

The stages of modern history coincide with the developmental phases of subjectivism. Now, the view that being is thinking is the fundamental tenet of this movement. In other words, we find there the contention that things are, in the final analysis, nothing but parts or states of the ego. And modern man has thought, loved, and struggled within the vast horizon produced on the basis of this view. In this context, the very idea which man has had of himself has taken shape. Leibniz says, for example, that man is a *petit Dieu* [little God]. The relative modesty displayed here is simply due to the fact that subjectivism had not yet achieved its acme in Leibniz. But Kant's imposing figure is placed at the very zenith of the unfolding of idealism. And he contends that man is the legislator of the universe. If we took just one more step, we would encounter Fichte, who transforms the ego into the *omnitudo realitatis* [the totality of reality], that is to say, into God. On the basis of the ego, and by virtue of its own creative acts, Fichte is to deduce the rest of the world. In fact, subjectivistic idealism has meant only one thing with greater or lesser clarity: the divinization of the ego, or that form of pantheism in which everything is God by virtue of the fact that each and every thing is a part of myself, since everything is in me, and my ego imbues the entire infinity of the universe with its own substance.

We have been educated during the Modern Age and in conformity with its principles, but at a time when, having fulfilled their historical mission, the age and its basic principles were beginning to collapse and dissolve. As in any other sector of life, a dissolution of this sort is not, of course, a case of mere annihilation, but rather a manner of preparing the way for new styles of living. As Hegel contended, every dissolution within the development of thought is a process of overcoming, and every form of overcoming is a way of preservation. And this is so because the new idea—as it surmounts the old one—comes to harbor the old one within itself forever, just as a larger quantity comprehends smaller ones. The newly emerging ideas are pregnant with their own mothers, an exact reversal of the situation in biological generation.

A decisive connection indeed exists between the radical changes affecting our way of understanding the ultimate problem—the relations between being and thought—and the possible variations in our manner of thinking, willing, and feeling anything else. (And this is so whether the radical changes are the causes of the variations or, as seems more likely, the chief symptoms of them.) No further consideration of this matter will be required by anyone who has a clear notion of such a connection.

The philosopher has no doubt that his mission today consists in undertaking, once more, the vast and infinite task of reshaping the very foundations of general consciousness according to a new plan, as well as attempting to resolve anew the primordial problem involved in the relations between being and thought. The questions to be faced are nothing less than those implied in redistributing areas of jurisdiction between subject and object. There is no sense in returning to the realism of the Ancients, but neither is it possible to remain within the boundaries established by the quid pro quo which is at the basis of subjectivism. We can have neither the subject subordinated to the object (as Aristotle does) nor the object subordinated to the subject (as Kant, in part, and Fichte, resolutely, do). What then? Perhaps Plato has a great deal to teach us; perhaps there are dimensions to his thought which have as yet neither produced effects nor met with any elaboration at all. Perhaps there is something in Plato which rises above the horizons of the Ancient world and, surmounting the Modern Age, addresses itself to us as a signal and a guiding star.

In any case, we should search after a new and equitable regimen by which to govern the relations between subject and object. And since we have alluded to the religious outcomes of ancient and modern philosophy, it may very well be permissible to say that our task would consist in learning to see subject and object as if they were like those divine beings whom the Etruscans called *Dii consentes*, the gods in reciprocity, and of whom they used to say that they could only be born and die together. Let us hope that the new climate of opinion announced by means of such gods is more propitious to Spain. Or, again, let us hope that Spain contributes to the discharge of the new task.

7

Word, sign, and object. Nominal definition.
Consciousness and soul. Object *A* and object *A'*.
Science as the "system of living reason." Consciousness as reference. The "natural" and reflexive attitudes of consciousness. Antithetical
judgments. The object "judgment" and the object "being a problem." Why is a judgment a
judgment? Absolute positivism versus partial
positivism. Acts of presentation, imagination,
and mere meaning-intending. The relationships
between such acts. Husserl's distinction.

IN THE LAST FEW LECTURES, we have dealt mainly with objects. An object—we said—was anything that can become
the terminus of consciousness, i.e., anything that exists for
me or is before me, or anything that I am aware of or refer
to. For now, expressions like "existing for me," "being before me," "my being aware of," "my referring to," and so
on will be taken as synonymous. All of them in fact can be
gathered under the more technical (albeit less flexible) term
"consciousness."

A word is a sign inviting us to direct or project ourselves
toward a certain given object. It may very well happen that
the same sign comes to denote different objects to different
people. If someone attempted to force others to use the sign
A exclusively to denote or refer to object *X*, we would have

to say that we were being faced only with an argument over words, taking "argument" here in its bad sense. Another case, however, involves more than a mere verbal exercise. Suppose I say that it does not matter to me which name or sign you select to denote object X. You can choose whichever word you like, provided only that you meet this requirement: that you refer to the same object as I, that you not mistake it for another, however similar the two may be. Language, or the system of signs employed for intellectual exchange in everyday life, is capable, of course, of successfully denoting common objects. In science, however, we are concerned with objects we do not usually deal with in everyday life. Moreover, the minimal essential requirement for scientific parlance is never to confuse one object with another, even if the difference between them is so small as to be negligible from a *pragmatic*, or *living*, point of view. In science we therefore need a language or system of signs which would be to everyday language as theoretical objects are to pragmatic things.[1] To begin with, a greater degree of accuracy would be required, and accuracy is contingent upon distinguishing things precisely. When I caution you, as I am about to do, not to confuse "consciousness" with "soul," let it be clearly understood that I couldn't care less whether you or I confuse such words as they sound to the ear, but I am greatly concerned with making sure that you do not confuse the *thing* called "consciousness" with the *thing* referred to as "soul."

But how can we avoid such a confusion? In principle, the only way to do so is to fix the value we assign to the signs we use, or, so to speak, the accuracy of their aim. For success in this enterprise, we must distinguish any two given signs—which in everyday employment direct or project consciousness to one and the same object—by means of other signs. This effort ought to be continued, and new signs introduced, until we are rid of confusion, and everyone can aim his thought at the same target. When we succeed, the result is the "nominal definition," which always begins with a phrase like "by *A* I understand. . . ." Expressions of this sort sound like parts of mere word games or verbal conflicts only to someone who has never reflected on the matter, that is to say, to one who does not know exactly what is being talked about. In adopting this attitude, he would only make his ignorance about the nature of words quite apparent, for he would be assuming that each of them is a mere noise, or *flatus vocis*, even though the sound profile of a word is the least important thing about it. Indeed, he would ignore the fact that exhibiting a sound profile is not even necessary, since being endowed with meaning is the essential property of a word. Now, meaning is precisely the instrumentality by which we are directed to, come to be related with, or engage in regarding this or that thing. But being directed to this or that is what is usually called thinking, and thinking is, in the final analysis, the general and only way of taking hold of things or realities that is available in Spain, on earth, or in the solar system of Alpha Centauri, either to us or to God himself. Accordingly, the process of fixing the value of signs, of engaging in verbal clarification, turns out to be an essential component of the mechanism needed to establish what things are, and the only means at our disposal to ensure that no two disputants argue only over words.

But let us leave this matter for a later occasion, when it will be fitting to expound the general theory of signs, of which words are only a special case. As a matter of fact, this subject is again in the foreground of scientific research. And yet, although this is not the right occasion to do so, we should make sure that our discussion of this matter—even if only in outline—does not appear as an oddity. If you agree that habits of thinking generally characteristic of science are rarely found in our country, you will also grant that habits of thinking which conform with philosophical methodology are almost nonexistent here. And the very small minority devoted tot his kind of investigation becomes aware of the difficulty at every turn, in the form of stumbling blocks and all manner of unpleasantness and vexation, among which not the least important is having to spend one's life defending one's work against commonplace objections and basic forms of ignorance.

But let us move along.

We shall not take "consciousness" as if it meant "soul." By "soul" I understand the real being which—[whether] endowed with spiritual or physiological attributes—we regard as the substrate of mental and conscious phenomena, just as we posit matter as the substrate of physical phenomena. When the biologist, observing the whole extent of nerve fibers under the microscope, says, as Bethe for one does,[2] that they intersect at a given point and form a knot, he is merely describing a phenomenon just as it is, precisely as it presents itself. When, on the contrary, a biologist asserts that such a nerve knot is a nerve *center*, the object so characterized is not just as we see it through the microscope. This object is not manifest; it is only supposed to be thus and so. To be a center is to perform a special function within the system of functions we hypothetically attribute to the nervous system. Such an object, as compared with the object as seen, has only a probable status. As compared with consciousness, "soul" is likewise hypothetical and probable.

Accordingly, we shall not gloss over the following basic consideration. When we attempt to explain an object A (e.g., light, or the set of all colors), what we are after is a sort of meta-reality lying behind the object (in this instance, behind the colors we see). Let us refer to such a meta-reality as A'. In keeping with our example, I could identify A' as a set of vibrations occurring in the ether. Our acceptance of A' permits us to reduce A (the colors) to the status of lawful phenomena. The vibrations taking place in the ether are

then the means we employ to explain colors to our satisfaction, and yet we must exercise caution, making sure to
regard the reality of vibrations only as secondary to the
reality of the seen but unexplained colors. The reason for
this distinction is quite simple. The reality assigned to the
vibrations of light is predicated on whether or not they.
explain the apparent, or phenomenal, colors, but the reality
of the colors is predicated on nothing at all. Phenomena are
absolutely manifest. They do not advance themselves as
being more than they appear to be, nor can they possibly
exceed what they seem to be. Accordingly, when we give
a correct description of a phenomenon, we have formulated
an absolute truth. As we shall see, a divine or infinite understanding—should there be one—would have to acknowledge that truth and take it as valid.

The matters under examination present themselves at this
point only as likely. And yet inherent in such probable
presentation is a principle of the highest rank, which will
have validity for the final ascertainment of such matters. I
mean the axiom according to which no explanatory truth
may have a retroactive effect on descriptive truths. In other
words, no proposition belonging in the sciences of reality
(for instance, the natural sciences) can exercise the slightest
influence on the phenomenological or purely descriptive sciences, such as logic, ontology, mathematics, and still other
disciplines which as yet are either not well known or not
invented at all, but which, among the newest fields of inquiry, I regard as exhibiting an unlimited fertility. Among
those which are not well known, I may mention the science
of "color geometry," which has nothing whatever to do with
physical or physiological optics. This discipline examines
the colors we see precisely as we see them, and yet discusses
them in terms of laws no less rigorous and evident than
those of mathematics. Among those which are hardly known,
I wish to refer to what I term the "system of living reason,"

which deals with a problem that is somewhat difficult to pose and that has not—as far as I know—been discovered until now. I mean, of course, that it has not so far been discovered *as such*, since obscure beginnings and traces of it have indeed been found or may still be scattered about in other sciences. They may have been dealt with, too, as part of that perspicuous sector of scientific knowledge recently gathered under the heading of *Weltanschauung* (the Idea of the World), or even under the still poorer or more absurd name "pragmatism." But let us forgo the tantalizing task of concretely and methodically presenting this "system of living reason," despite the fact that it has unparalleled importance to me, as the child always has in the eyes of his own father.

Our urgent task consists in learning to appreciate that "consciousness" is only one of the sides or faces of a phenomenon, of something which lies absolutely manifest. And we are not to speak here of just any phenomenon; we aim to discuss only a fundamental one, indeed the phenomenon par excellence. And this is so because every possible definite *quid*, everything about which we may say "it is," or "it exists," or "it is there," is *ipso facto* included in that reference which is intrinsic to consciousness—i.e., in the fundamental phenomenon by which a subject is directed to an object (or, vice versa, in the event by which an object finds itself apprehended by a subject). Anything of which we are able to speak, or even relate to in ways prior to those of speech, is already an object. But if this is so, it already exhibits— among its inherent features—that most general trait which consists in finding itself before me or being the terminus of consciousness. Once this is grasped, we can appreciate the unparalleled difficulty we experience whenever we attempt to describe the phenomenon of consciousness. Here we are confronted with the greatest of paradoxes, for the most difficult thing to see turns out to be that which is encountered or present everywhere. Suppose that everything in the world were blue; suppose further that we could relate to nothing which was not blue. In that situation, we would have to perform the highest feats of abstraction to come to the realization that something blue actually exists and that its nature is precisely being blue. Given the presence of blue everywhere and our inability to miss it anywhere, such a chromatic quality would be unstressed and would remain, so to speak, in the background. Precisely the opposite is characteristic of the differences between things. Whatever is present in something but absent in something else seems on its own strength to become noticeable to us.

Now then, the phenomenon of conscious reference is the universal medium in which float all other phenomena; it penetrates into the ultimate recesses of all real and possible objects.

Our natural disposition or state of mind inclines us to deal with the objects, objectives, or goals toward which our consciousness is directed or on which it eventually rests, but does not allow for our paying attention to our own consciousness of them. Men live by busying themselves with objects and only with objects, whether they be practical men, physicists, or mathematicians. Only for the noologist and the psychologist is the consciousness of objects itself a habitual object of interest. The rest of mankind are engaged in thinking, willing, and feeling things, but there is no reason in the world why they should toil their way after the events of thinking, willing, or feeling things. They do not need to do any such thing; they are not called to that enterprise. The lyrical poet lives wrapped up in himself, his inner conditions, his states of sadness or enthusiasm, but does not busy himself with his own manner of self-consciousness, with his way of feeling sadness or enthusiasm. And this is as it should be. We ought not then to be surprised to hear Goethe express his strong dislike for psychological and epistemological considerations. So far as the natural attitude of consciousness is concerned, he was perfectly right in saying:

> Truly speaks the man who asserts
> that no one knows how it is we think;
> when think we do,
> everything is as a gift.[3]

Whenever I open my eyes, the first objects I actually encounter are those out there ready to give themselves as presents to me. Only later, after I am done with the objects I see, may I come to find a new kind of object: my act of seeing. And I may accomplish this by returning from the objects to my own self. Sadness is present altogether in what I call my ego or my soul, and so much so that it imbues it throughout, giving it, so to speak, a special coloring, just as bluing, cast into a pond, colors it through and through. Only by starting with my own sadness and then proceeding inward, only by turning my back on sadness, can I come to discover my consciousness of sadness, a new object so different from sadness itself that we cannot say of it that it is sad or that it may ever become so.

The natural attitude of consciousness is that by which we open up toward the objects themselves. Accordingly, only by twisting or turning about our natural attitude, only by way of reflection, can we encounter our consciousness of objects as such.

Herein originates the difficulty many people experience with the philosophical and psychological sciences. Thinking is not a "natural" object for thinking. In fact, a not inconsiderable number of philosophers deny that thinking ever can become an object for itself. This thesis, however, is somewhat tricky, for, mind you, whenever the philosophers speak in such a fashion, they indeed demonstrate that they know there is "thinking" in the world and, further, that its nature is *such* that no one can ever come to know what it is, i.e., that no one can consider it or think about it. But if they are correct, how have they been able to derive all such knowledge? A different view seems more likely. I mean the contention that thinking can become an object only when it corresponds to a special attitude of consciousness, one which, in a certain sense, we could characterize as "unnatural." This would be the philosophical attitude, which is defined by its proper object just as physics and biology are defined by theirs. In opposing philosophical, or reflexive, consciousness to "natural" consciousness, we must be most careful not to claim for the former any super-natural status. And yet this has been the idiosyncratic obsession of philosophers, who, like all other beings, tend to represent God to themselves as if He were a superlative magnification of their own natures. Thus Aristotle says: *estí nóesis noéseos* [(it) is a thinking of thinking].[4] [According to him, then,] such is the being of God. Aristotle thus transforms God into some kind of philosopher, indeed a philosopher carried to the superlative degree. It is no surprise, then, to find H[erbert] Spencer claiming later that He is in fact a monumental engineer.

As you may remember, we were concerned with the acts or modalities of consciousness, with the means by which we become conscious of the various kinds of objects. In fact, we sought to match every sort of object with the kind of act, or modality of consciousness, by which it is disclosed. Now then, such acts constitute consciousness, the domain of which we have spoken today. And only with great difficulty can consciousness be separated from its own termini or goals—the objects themselves. I hope the word "act" does not turn into a special stumbling block for you. Once you have become accustomed to scrutinizing the modalities of consciousness, you will find them to be, so to speak, char-acteristically spontaneous motions, i.e., performances of some kind of activity. If I disengage what I want from my wanting of it, or what I perceive from my perceiving of it, I am left with two different sorts of "something," namely, with my wanting and with my perceiving. [Take for instance the first case.] Such I can only describe by saying that it is that activity of mine concerning a thing to which we normally refer by means of the word "wanting," for it is neither identical with the performer of the act of wanting (me myself), nor with the thing wanted by me.

But let us return now to what, from our point of view, is a pressing matter.

We argued before that, properly speaking, a problem ex-ists only when we find a pair of antithetical judgments. The opposition, between, say, "a rose's being-white" and "a rose's not-being-white" is not, strictly speaking, a problem. The two characterizations are simply two different structural objects or complex things. In other words, we just encounter two entities which co-exist without excluding one another, one being positive and the other negative. Such is the case too with "red" and "yellow." We do find a problem, how-ever, in situations conveyed by expressions like "whether or not a rose is white." Among problems continually hound-ing and plaguing us, I could mention the following: whether or not God exists, whether or not a living organism is a machine, and whether or not democracy is an adequate form of government. Now then, in every instance of this kind we come across a pair of antithetical judgments. And it is judgments of this sort which exclude one another, not the structural objects which they refer to or judge about.

Accordingly, we need to look into the makeup of the object "judgment" if indeed we are to identify the special factor responsible for its compatibility with the object "being a problem." In fact, the answer would indicate why the object "judgment" is not merely compatible with the object "being a problem," but even attracts the latter to itself.

What, then, is a judgment? I do not for a moment hesitate to say that the lack of progress observed since Aristotle's achievements concerning this matter was a source of chagrin until just a few years ago. Even today we are merely beginning to make our way toward the understanding of the complex structure of judgment. Here we have a case exemplifying the co-operation which must exist among the sciences, lest they become sterile and stagnant. A usual complaint among linguists is that we are not at present clear about the nature of syntactical structures. But how could it be otherwise, since the philosopher—whether he calls himself noologist or psychologist—has not yet seriously attempted to give a formulation to the anatomy of judgment? I do not deny that there are reasons and even justifications for this sorry state of affairs, as for example in the pressing need for the establishment of laws governing the truth of judgments, as the decisive means for knowledge which they are. That is why philosophers have devoted great efforts to the analytical examination of true judgments, that is to say, to the determination of the logical and critical aspects of judgment. But they have left the rest of the makeup of a judgment untouched, and have not submitted to scrutiny whatever is responsible precisely for its being a judgment, whether true or false.

This is a difficult and most intricate subject, and yet I believe we can arrive at some conclusions about it, provided we restrict our considerations to that which is strictly relevant to our concerns. To begin with, we find that we refer to two different objects in any judgment of the form "A is B" (e.g., "The rose is white"). In our example, such objects would be "the rose" and "white." And yet we cannot say of either, or of the whole they form together, that they make the object of the judgment itself. Each such item, and the whole they constitute, may become the objects of other acts of consciousness. For instance, "the rose" and "white" may be *seen*, *imagined*, or *merely intended*. And in those three ways they can be given to us either separately or together.

I can see a "rose" that is red, and at another time and place I can see "white." Then again I can see something which is both a rose and white. All of this is quite familiar. Still, there is another manner of being conscious of something, one which occurs more frequently and yet is less well known to us. I mean the act or modality of consciousness I have called mere intending.

I referred to this event of consciousness in a previous lecture. Now, given its importance, it is worth our while to renew our effort at reflection. I can put the question in the following way, so that you may come to see the nature of mere intending in the most direct fashion.[5]

Any object (say, the monastery at El Escorial) may be regarded by the subject from the standpoints of three different attitudes. That is to say, it may appear or be before him in three different manners. Let us examine them.

First: I am now at El Escorial, and I am looking at the monastery directly. In this situation, the building is present to me. I encounter the monastery itself right before me. Here is the shortest possible distance that may exist between the object and me. This form of givenness I shall call presence.

Second: I can look at an engraving of the monastery. In this case, only some printed matter, not the building itself, is right before me. And yet we would also have to say that the monastery evidently is before me, since the engraving present is a representation of the building. In this experience, I refer to the monastery by means of the engraving; the building somehow looms up before my grasp. But if I examine the way the object now appears to me, in contrast to the manner of presence, I discover that it shows up by way of absence, the only thing actually present being the image of the object. We have thus identified a second manner of establishing a distance between ourselves and the object. We find a more glaring example of the resulting manner of absence in the mode of consciousness we call memory. What I remember is always something past. To expect the object itself to become present when I remember it would be absurd indeed; strangely, it is before me by way of absence, as a past thing or occurrence. Absence, then, is not a negative characteristic but an apparent, unmediated feature, one which is certainly as positive in nature as pure presence, and yet cannot be mistaken for it. Absence is not merely a not-being-found-there, but a positive being-absent, a simple representation.

Memorial presentations and images are cases of a manner of being conscious of objects which still has not received the detailed study it deserves, despite pledges to do so which have been made by various phenomenologists and which have been outstanding now for several years. In this lecture course, I shall have the opportunity to expound the results of my investigations on this matter. I have been greatly interested in it, because it is—no more and no less—the level of experience at which the plastic arts, without exception, are given. We cannot seriously develop an aesthetic theory unless we make the arduous effort to clarify the nature of the consciousness of images. Every painting or sculpture is an image, and in every image two objects interpenetrate: one which is present, namely, the colors and the lines on canvas, or the volume or the body of the marble piece; and another which is absent, namely, whatever the color or the marble represents. Now, neither object, regarded in isolation, can be taken as a work of beauty. That work is rather the conjunction of both, when given in essential reciprocity and as indissolubly coupled.

Third: It would seem that besides presence and absence,

there could be no other distance at which the object could be given or situated with respect to ourselves. And yet those of you who have never seen either the monastery at El Escorial or a picture of it were able to understand me when I spoke of that object a moment ago. I think if we could understand only what we have seen or imagined, we would never understand one another, since what is seen or imagined cannot be conveyed by itself. The act of conveying anything to another is effected by means of signs or words.

Now then, to confuse understanding with knowing would be a great error. Take the following example. When I say "infinitesimal calculus," those of you who do not know infinitesimal calculus nevertheless understand me. Someone could retort that, strictly speaking, you do know something about it, for when I say "infinitesimal calculus," you say to yourself something like, "a mathematical discipline, or a part of mathematics." Understanding the one phrase, then, would amount to substituting the other for it. But such a prudent and plain observation can be countered by another: if indeed we could make substitutions like "a part of mathematics" for "infinitesimal calculus," with one phrase exactly replacing the other, and if, further, the intelligence or understanding of words consisted precisely in that act of substitution, then the existence of so many words would be pointless, for if one expression perfectly translated into another, we would need one and only one in every case. But, after all, it could be that in fact we characteristically display such a serious lack of economy in our conduct. (And yet, as opposed to this eventuality, which is only a matter of probability, we can insist upon what was said just previously.)

But the serious difficulty here is that the phrase "a part of mathematics" (or any impressive array of similar phrases) cannot, strictly speaking, be substituted for "infinitesimal calculus." Projective geometry, for example, is also "a part of mathematics," and yet it is not to be confused with infinitesimal calculus. One of the great many characteristics of the object "infinitesimal calculus" certainly is that of being "a part of mathematics"; yet by the expression "infinitesimal calculus" we obviously understand not just any part of mathematics, but precisely this unique, unmistakable branch.

The person who does not know the monastery at El Escorial finds himself in a similar predicament. He knows about other monasteries; he is also aware that a town named El Escorial exists in the province of Madrid. But, exactly in the context so formed, we recognize the oddity of the thing, namely, that when this person hears what we say, he understands that we are not referring to the monasteries he has seen, but precisely to that definite, unique, particular, individual building which he has not seen.

Consequently, the act of understanding words is an instance of that kind of conscious phenomenon by which we find ourselves engaged in commerce with an object of which we know nothing, an object indeed which is neither present nor available to us by means of fragment or representation, emblem or image. In order to acknowledge Dulcinea's incomparable beauty, the merchants asked first to see the woman's portrait, even if it had been only as small as a graint of wheat. In order to acknowledge the fact, then, they wanted first to know it, and acting thus they did just what was right. But perhaps Don Quixote wanted less; perhaps he only wanted his words and the longing of his heart to be understood.

At first glance, this phenomenon is irritating indeed. Like the merchants, the so-called positivists and the sensualists in the field of psychology fly into a rage when confronted with phenomena of this sort,[6] since they do not easily fit their theoretical accounts, for how can it be possible to deal consciously with something, to become aware of anything, if we possess nothing of it and nothing belonging to it is a content of our consciousness? "Content of consciousness" is an awful terminological expression which I have not hitherto employed, and which I now present as somebody else's utterance. Eventually, on a more fitting occasion, we shall deal with such a term, and I shall attempt to show how the sterility of present-day psychology derives from it almost entirely.

Let us agree that the phenomenon we are now dealing with is irritating. If I were in charge of the universe, I would remove such a feature altogether, as a good deed in behalf of the sensualist theories of consciousness. But until this comes to pass, we have no choice but to prefer the evidence available for the phenomenon—as yet to be comprehended—over problematical theories, in the light of which the said phenomenon is incomprehensible. It may very well be that, as Homer used to think, Achilles and Hector were born just to have their deeds sung by Homer, but the indubitable fact is that phenomena have not been made to fit our theories; on the contrary, theories are made to fit phenomena.

For myself, I could now present the alpha and omega of my logical and methodological convictions by proposing an anticipatory, summary formula, but not without first acknowledging that such condensed expressions naturally tend to be inexact. With this reservation in mind, I would argue *for absolute positivism and against any partial form thereof*. Any conclusions, theories, and systems are true, provided that *everything* said in them finds its origin in the direct insight into the objects or phenomena themselves.

Now, I do not see "the number encompassing all numbers," "the star farthest removed from the earth," or "the first amoeba that ever was," nor do I succeed in forming representations thereof. But I indeed see—and, since I do, I also know—that I understand such names. Moreover, I also see and know that by means of them I refer to certain

unique and unmistakable objects which are not present before me and are not even represented by me as absent. In
fact, they give themselves to me just, precisely, and only
as "objects to which I refer." Above and beyond presence
and absence, then, we have the modality of reference by
virtue of which I find in myself not the object in question,
but only my reference to it.

In my opinion, we should bring certain everyday words
back to the status of technical terms, and use them to express
this strange fashion we have of relating to objects—a fashion
that is strange if viewed in the light of familiar theory, but—
as we shall see—is the most common manner that consciousness has of relating to objects. I mean such words as
"mention" *(mención)* and "mentioning" *(mentar).* Having
something "mentioned" to me, or "brought to mind," does
not necessarily imply that I in fact see or imagine it. Rather,
the sense of these expressions allows for the possibility that
objects have other, more subtle or distant ways of placing
themselves before us. At least, the sense of such terms does
not exclude this possibility in principle.

Let us then agree to avail ourselves of the vague extension
characteristic of such words in spontaneous speech, and let
us do so by restricting them to denoting only what is excluded from our experience of perceiving and representing.
Accordingly, we shall refer to those events by which an
object is rendered present to us as acts of *perceiving* or *presentation*, [to those in which an object is given to us in the
manner of absence as acts of *representation* or *imagining*,][7] and
to those others in which an object is given by way of allusion
and reference as acts of *mentioning* or *bringing to mind*.

And now let us proceed, setting aside endless sequences
of questions to which we cannot even pause to give expression. As an example, let me point to the subject of the
relations between the three modalities of givenness I have
identified, and let me raise just a few questions. Is it possible

to perceive an object without at once bringing it to mind? Or is the act of bringing an object to mind the elemental way we have of being conscious, one which would be, so to speak, wrapped in and enclosed by every act of consciousness, no matter which? Or take another subject: Would the mere bringing to mind of an object not be the essential act by which what we usually call meaning comes to be fulfilled? Would speaking and understanding not amount to bringing an object to mind? Could we not find in the distinction we have elaborated, which is apparently so inconsequential, the very key to construct a whole new philosophy of language? Could it not be that the opposition I have implied between acts of perceiving and representing on the one hand, and acts of bringing to mind on the other, constitutes a more fitting and exact formulation than [Edmund] Husserl's own opposition between between acts of "mere or *empty* meaning-intending" and acts of "meaning-fulfillment," that is to say, between acts in which I refer to something and acts in which something is given to me directly and immediately?[8] Now, to gauge the importance of this matter, it would suffice to note that since 1901, every philosophical position revolves around, opposes, or defends Husserl's distinction. For it may very well be possible to define learning or coming to know the truth, so as to give it expression in an ultimate and most clear and concrete fashion, by saying that it constitutes an attempt to find the act which would fulfill a mere meaning-intending, inasmuch as what was only brought to mind in the mere intending would be given in the act of fulfillment. But in that case, we would discover that the old, venerable, and enigmatic "concepts"—to use here for the first time that sacramental word proper to philosophical discourse—turn out to be, after all, nothing but acts of bringing to mind. And then we would be so fortunate as to require no longer the term "concept," which for centuries has been lodged in the innermost recesses of the meditations carried out by philosophers and which, as a would-be vessel sunken at the bottom of the sea, has been overlaid by algae and seaweed, by judgment and prejudgment.

(After the discussion, we proceeded into the analysis of attribution and began the analysis of judgment, both of which will be summarized in the following lecture.)[9]

8

A description of appearances; objectivating acts. A critical examination of the four kinds of [theses about] the structure of judging. First kind: judging *qua* synthesis. Second kind: judging *qua* identification. Third kind: judging *qua* inherence. Pure grammar. Fourth kind: judging *qua* acknowledgment, whether positive or negative. The intentionality of consciousness.

IN THE PREVIOUS LECTURE, we were able to see that we could introduce a differentiation among the modalities of consciousness, one resulting in the distinction between acts by virtue of which we are confronted with objects and those by means of which consciousness acts upon objects. Such a discrimination was possible even when we set aside the regions of volition and feeling within consciousness itself, a procedure which left us only with the kind of conscious experience we called intellectual, a vague characterization indeed, but sufficient for our purposes now. The acts of perceiving, imagining, and bringing to mind coincide in that all three merely offer us objects, even as they differ in the special way of relating objects to us which is proper to each.

Let us at no time lose sight of the fact that we are referring here only to phenomena; let us remain aware of this point in everything we are saying. Accordingly, when I contend that some conscious acts merely offer us objects, while others act on the objects, I mean only to describe or give expres-

sion to certain apparent characteristics as they actually present themselves. Likewise, when we study volitional
phenomena and perhaps say that certain motions present
themselves as originating in the ego, or as if set going or
caused by the core of our psyches, it is to be understood
that we are only describing what appears, precisely as it
appears. Formulations of this sort would remain intact and
would preserve their truth value, even if later findings were
to convince us that the ego is nothing but a nexus of physiological states which, owing to a blind, natural causality,[1]
succeed one another, a discovery which would indeed deny
the "real" existence of such would-be voluntary movements.
And this would be the case with our formulations because
we have limited ourselves to describing appearances, and
appearances are, as I have said before, beyond question.

Now, we characterized as *objectivating* acts those events
wherein objects are merely offered to us. Over against them,
we noted the existence of relational, connective, articulating,
or *synthetical* acts. Undisturbed until [Franz] Brentano's inspired innovations of 1879 [actually 1874], tradition had
taken judging to be an act of synthesis, what Plato and
Aristotle called *symplokhé*. In his *Psychology from an Empirical
Standpoint*, Brentano tries to show that synthesis is not at
all essential to the act of judging. The question is too complex for us even to attempt to develop and resolve it here.
For our purposes, it will just do to find a first clear understanding of judging.

Let us review very briefly the main theses which have
been advanced about the definition of judging or, so to
speak, about its anatomical structure. We can reduce them
all to four kinds.[2]

First: Judging is the act of combining or dividing two
representations or (as is commonly said) two concepts. This
theory, which is the most obvious and the oldest, may help
us to realize how easily the part is mistaken for the whole

when mental phenomena are under examination. The act of joining representations may very well be involved in every act of judging,[3] but, even if this is so, there are certainly acts of combining which are not acts of judging. "Peter and John," for example, is the formula expressing the outcome of an act of combination, and yet it is not a judgment. However, when I say "Peter is clever," I accomplish something above and beyond joining two objects, something missing in "Peter and John." By the latter formula, we simply give expression to an act of collecting. That is all. Nothing can be so ruinous to logic and psychology as turning judging into the universal form of acts of synthesis, those acts which, by contrast with perceiving and imagining, constitute what we ordinarily call thinking. That is not so: adding, comparing, etc. are also acts of thinking, and yet they are not acts of judging.

Second: Judging consists in *identifying* or equating two representations. When we compared the expressions "Peter and John" and "Peter is clever," we were able to recognize an essential difference between them. In fact, we discovered the existence of a *plus* in favor of the latter formula. Theories of the second sort propose to account for this *plus* by means of an argument like this: what in judging exceeds the mere joining of two representations lies in the fact that we note an identity or an equality between the two. This identity is the very meaning of the copula: "is" signifies "is identical with." Judging would then be an act of identifying. By judging I find in Peter something identical with cleverness. The Neo-Kantian schools as a whole and other related movements adopt this theoretical position and explore it in depth. To this kind of explanation belongs [Christoph] Sigwart's conception of *In-eins-setzung*, the notion of "positing in unity," but so also does the far-reaching doctrine advanced by [Hermann] Cohen and [Paul] Natorp, who turn the act of judging into the key to all knowledge (following in this, to

be sure, the spirit of Kant). I do not seek to deny the element
of truth in this position: I defer to it and leave it intact. And
yet to understand it would require of us more time and
effort than we presently have at our disposal, for it is possibly the most difficult of all philosophical positions.

Let us consider only that aspect of such theories which
prevents them from being of use to us in the definition of
judging. Identity and equality—for our purposes we can
employ either one—are forms of relation, but only two such
forms among many. Two things may be related to each
other by way of equality, but may also be related as the
part is to the whole, or by way of inherence (as when one
is the property of the other), or in other manners as well.
When I say "This rose is from Valencia," I am not aware
of asserting any identity between this rose and the wide and
fertile plains of Valencia, a claim which on its face would
be absurd. At best, by such words I would be declaring
that I realize that such a flower is found in the gardens of
the region. When, pointing to a coin, Jesus said "This is
Caesar's," he meant to signify a relationship of belonging-
ness between the coin and the authority of Caesar. Finally,
when I say "The rose is white," I do not assert that "rose"
and "white" are one and the same. We can further verify
that it is not possible to reduce judgment to the relationship
of identity or equality by observing the change of meaning
undergone by any judgment for which a genuine identity-
judgment is substituted. "A is A" and "A is identical with
A" do not mean the same thing. The fact that A is identical
with A is perchance the foundation, reason, or motive leading me to judge that A is A, but I do not mean the same
thing in both instances.

These brief remarks concerning the second thesis about
the nature of the act of judging will have to do for now.
Let us turn to another sort of explanation.

Third: It is here that my preceding points are to be validated. The theories belonging in this group simply extend the scope of those of the second kind. In fact, Sigwart and expecially Cohen, Natorp, and more recently [Emil] Lask would have to be included in both groups.[4] According to this extension of the second position, judging would consist, to be sure, in noticing an identity, but not an identity between things (such as "rose" and "white"); rather it would exist between such things on the one hand and the concept of relation on the other. "The rose is white" would thus be an elliptical expression for an act wherein we identify the real situation in which rose-and-white are found together with the concept of inherence: "rose" and "white" constitute a case of inherence. We encounter the same situation when we substitute "A and B are causally connected" for "A is the cause of B." As one can gather, the view that the subject of the judgment is pre-conceptual (say, a perception) and that the predicate is intelligible (i.e., a concept or a category by means of which the real is comprehended) is essential to these theories. According to them the act of judging exercises the highest rational authority, or, as Plato would say, it "bestows rational or intelligible being" on realities (i.e., *génesis eis ousía*).

Not even for a moment will I allow myself to cast a doubt on the usefulness and profound sense characteristic of this opinion as part of a given epistemological theory. But now we are not examining knowledge, that is to say, the question concerning the possibility that our thinking, a subjective affair, would successfully grasp any entity taken absolutely and trans-subjectively. In other words, we are not analyzing here the problems pertaining, for example, to the determination of how it is that the great and resplendent stars obey and subject themselves to our judgments about them, and that entities endowed with such power and encircled by such mystery nevertheless allow themselves to be tamed by the lowly astronomers of earth. So magnificent and sacred is this subject for man that he may find in what Kant called the *Faktum* of astronomy the very firm support on which to stand and haughtily face the infinite and mysterious Universe.

But we are not concerned with this question at the moment, for here we are interested only in the event of judging as such—as it occurs in ourselves, or as an act present to our consciousness, quite apart from considerations as to whether such an act would succeed in grasping transcendent reality.

Having thus delimited my subject, I might nevertheless raise a great number of objections against this third kind of theory, but for my purposes, only one will be sufficient now. I formulate it as follows: without exception, all such relationships of equality, inherence, part-to-whole, etc. may be expressed, and therefore thought, without involving any act of judging. "Caesar's coin," "the white rose," "the rose from Valencia," "clever Peter," and the like are all [connected with] acts of attribution and not [with] acts of judging. As you know, the copula "is" first forced us to look for something beyond the mere joining of "Peter and John," a *plus* which was then variously interpreted as "is identical with," "is inherent in," "is the property of," "is the cause of," etc. And yet the copula "is" does not appear in the expressions now under scrutiny, while equality, inherence, etc. are contained therein. I am not saying, then, that judging does not involve a joining of representations, or an identification, or any other form of relationship. But I do certainly assert that acts of attribution may also involve such things. Consequently, when we place the diminutive word "is" against a background of attributive acts, we come to realize that it signifies something above and beyond what such acts mean. "The white rose" and "The rose is white" do not exhaust the meaning of "is." Would it be correct, perchance, to take "the red tulip" and "The tulip is red" as having one and the same meaning? Proof that this is not so is found in the fact that I can truly say, "The red tulip is not" or "does not exist," or "There is no such thing." If the two expressions had identical meaning, the mere joining of "the red tulip" with the expression "is not" would cancel both "the red tulip" and "The tulip is red" [, but this is not the case].

Let us now attempt to summarize what has been said thus far, so as to achieve greater clarity on these matters. On the one hand, we have the primordial modalities or acts of consciousness by means of which objects are posited for us. I mean the acts of perceiving, imagining, and bringing to mind. On the other hand, we find secondary performances of consciousness which act upon those primordial acts—or, more exactly, on the objects which are simply given therein. By virtue of such secondary acts we attribute one object to another, collect or compare objects, and so on. Through these acts new qualities arise in objects, as when, for example, an object is seen as a substance and another as something which inheres in it, or an object is seen as a part of another which is the whole, or objects are regarded as identical, as equal, as forming part of a manifold, and so on and so forth. In the secondary acts attention is not focused on one singular object, but seemingly splits itself in two and affixes itself on two objects at once. This is why they are called acts of synthesis, why they articulate one object with another.

Moreover, I must remark that all such acts—whether primordial or secondary—can be performed without having to be expressed. I can see that cabinet, and then immediately perform an act [of thinking] which would consist not in perceiving but in explaining the always simple content of perception. And this can take place without my giving expression to such an act, whether by inner or outer word. For example, I can distinguish the various parts of the cabinet, (its top and bottom, its right and left sides), its color, its shape, etc. Even though everything involved in this is thinking proper, I can do it all in the most perfect external and internal silence. Expressive acts (the word and the phrase) constitute still another stratum of performance, one which casts upon the silent acts a finespun and nearly transparent tissue that adapts itself to their bodies and fits their limbs. And yet this effort does not give expression to every one of our acts, or to each of their parts and components. When the opportunity arises, we shall see that language—our medium of expression—transcribes our acts after its own fashion, just as our acts of thinking re-form or de-form the things or objects we think about, introducing into them characteristics which they would not possess in and of themselves. Take for instance the fact that a word is always general in nature, even when it is a proper name. Words, then, transform our acts into generalities, even though every one of them is unique. Pure or general grammar is the study of generality and other features of language: it is the discipline which engages in the a priori determination of the essential characteristics of language as such. Each particular language then adds its own idosyncratic contributions to our ways of expression, above and beyond the essential traits belonging to any language. To use a readily available example, we can say that it is proper to English and German to place the adjective before the noun. I wonder whether variations of this sort affect only the domain of expression or also render manifest special ways of thinking. Here a vast field opens up for productive research in which linguist and psychologist may collaborate.

In my view, making these remarks was important precisely to remove again the suspicion that in distinguishing between "the white rose" and " The rose is white" I might have been concerned with a mere phonetic difference. Not at all. I am not interested in the sound difference resulting from the presence or absence of "is" in such complex expressions, but I am interested in the observable difference in sense. In my opinion, both meanings are entirely identical except for an aspect which has to do with the copula "is." I would go as far as to contend that we have to rehabilitate the use of the concepts "subject" and "predicate," a position out of fashion today, for, as many present-day logicians and psychologists argue, Aristotle took such notions not from intellectual reality but from grammar. I believe that subject and predicate are essential functions of attributive acts, not merely the means to give expression to such acts. I can no doubt invert the word order in an expression like "the white rose," but whatever the order, one member of the expression will have one function to perform and the other a different function. The rose, always and in every language, will be the actor who, in the comedy which the expression constitutes, is the protagonist, or functions as the substrate to which something or other is attributed. In brief: it will play the role of substantive or subject, while white will always be billed as adjective or predicate. You can accordingly see that not even having a subject and a predicate is, in my opinion, a feature exhibited only in judgment. We find these in every attribution, in the guise of substantive and adjective.

What is then left which may correspond to the copula "is," if "the rose," "white," and the objective relationship between them (the white's belonging to the rose) are all already contained in the mere attribution "the white rose"? What can have remained unexpressed, since the objects involved and their relationships appear to have been exhausted by our analysis?

We have cornered, so to speak, the unruly term "is," which we use so often and which is, nevertheless, so resistant to disclosing its specific and genuine secret. But now, after so much insistent effort on our part, perhaps just a prick more will make the copula "is" burst open and yield its essence. Let us then turn our attention to the next way of theoretically accounting for the acts of judging.

Fourth: Let us not forget that the phenomenon of consciousness is for us something different from everything else, inasmuch as reference to objects was found among its features or characteristics. In any phenomenon other than consciousness, we meet with things in the process of becoming related with one another, as when, say, thing *A* collides with thing *B* in space. But there's the rub: we never discover that any one of the things involved in such relationships actually consists in the event of referring to another. Even if we regarded the very happening of a collision as a somewhat harsh modality of reciprocity, the things involved would always present themselves as being something more, something which pre-existed the collision. Now then, consciousness is not something which contains a reference to something else, but rather is the very act of referring itself, of bearing within its bosom what is intrinsically other than itself. In brief: nothing but consciousness consists in having an object, in becoming aware of something. This ultimate and primordial feature of consciousness has been called "intentionality," a suggestive term once employed by the Scholastics being thus brought back to life. Husserl indicates that whenever we use the term "consciousness," we should understand it as meaning "consciousness of. . . ."[5] Accordingly, every consciousness would be the consciousness of something.

On the one hand, it is to our advantage here to be reminded once more of this fact, which I have referred to so often. Insofar as it is a modality of consciousness, judging must have as its correlate an object which is its appropriate counterpart. Were we not able to point to an object which would be the proper correlate of the act, we would have to deny that judging has any specific nature and hence that an act of this kind exists at all. We would be rejecting the possibility that an act of this sort could constitute itself as a genuine and distinct modality among the many modalities of consciousness.

On the other hand, it seems to me that we have already exhausted the whole field of possible objects. Consequently, the copula "is" appears to have been rejected for its would-be post as object: we cannot assign it either to the rose or to the white of the rose or to the attribution of one to the other. Its status is like that of a shot into the air.

In one of his most recent books, [Theodor] Lipps makes the following perceptive remark:

> The relationships established between my consciousness and whatever is the terminus thereof seem to constitute a many-sided dialogue between myself and the object. First of all, I address myself to something, as when, say, I open my eyes. And, owing to this event, the thing in question becomes an object for me, or turns into my object. Then I address myself again to what is already my object, and subject it to scrutiny. Or equivalently stated: I relate it to other objects, I compare it with others, I distinguish it from them, I assign it a place in some order or other together with various objects, and so on. And as soon as I do this, the object seemingly revolts against me, as if it were addressing itself to me and pressing a demand on me. Then, in response to such demands, I adopt the special comportment of acknowledging or refusing them.[6]

Accordingly, as I compare this cabinet to that other, the former presses its demand on me that I acknowledge its equality to the latter.

Lipps's statements offer us some clues as to the meaning of the copula. There seems to be no real difference in material content between "the white rose" and "The rose is white." When we utter the copula "is," we do not add any material component [to what we already had]; we simply acknowledge, so to speak, a demand placed on us by the objects in question. In other words, we set before ourselves the task of determining the validity or invalidity of the demand.

And this is what theories of the fourth kind assert: judging is the act by which the validity of the judgment is assented to or dissented from, is approved or disapproved of, or is positively or negatively acknowledged.

Accordingly, judging appears to us as occurring within a new dimension of consciousness. Furthermore, the object of the act of judging appears to belong to a different dimension as well. Being is not another part of the object, as "white" for example is. Rather it is its value, that is to say, that which does not correspond to being seen, thought, compared, and so on, but is the correlate of acknowledgment.

(The act of referring consists in allowing admission to a demand or an imposition.

The iridescent meaning of the copula "is": "reality" on the side of the object and, on the side of the subject, the actuality of "belief." Our act of referring [to something] is an "attitude."

Brentano and the non-synthetical [understanding of judging].

[Wilhelm] Windelband and [Heinrich] Rickert[, on the other hand, are for the understanding of judging as] synthesis.

The "fact."

2 plus 2 are 4. [We mean here] neither 2 nor 4, but a [logical] necessity which seems to hover over it.[7]

The moral and aesthetic imperative.

The "ought."

"2 + 2 = 4" *exhibits validity*.

"[Axiology] or the Philosophy of *Value*.")

9

A review: truth and object.

THE PRECEDING LECTURES have served as an introduction leading us close to a land characterized by sudden turns of fortune, and especially to the greatest shift that may take place in the sphere of knowledge, namely, to doubt.

Let us briefly pose again the problem which concerns us, and let us do so precisely in the way it presented itself to us.

Truth and falsity constitute characters attributable only to objects of one special sort: acts performed by the conscious subject. As you remember, "object" was a term I employed to signify that which, strictly speaking, we can refer to, that which can become the terminus of consciousness. We can certainly refer to a stone or a star, but we can refer to an act of thinking or feeling as well.

What sense could there be to talking about a false star? Things can be neither true nor false. Expressions in ordinary language like "a false jewel," "a false friend," and so on, make us see even more clearly that it is impossible to attribute falsity directly to "jewel" or "friend." Strictly speaking, it is not the jewel which labors under falsity, but rather the act of judging, the act of the subject who judged this thing to be a jewel (or this man to be a friend), while in fact it is not.

We are agreed, then, that only objects which are acts of consciousness can be characterized by truth and falsity. But even this is not exactly the case. We can apply these determinations to only one sector within the entire province of conscious acts, since it is evident that a volition, or act of willing [for example], cannot possibly be either true or false. A false volition is just like a false jewel.

Falsity pertains not to the volitional act, but to the subject who thought that the act in question was a real volition, and not a fictive one.

On fictive inner life: Inner sense is more likely to be subject to illusion (e.g., to fictive sadness or fictive enthusiasm) than outer sense is. [It is like having] a toothache in the heart.

In the sphere of the modalities of consciousness, only noetic acts are t[rue] or f[alse]. Noetic acts are those performances by means of which consciousness refers to objects as such. [It is] difficult to define a *noetic* [act]. [We can do so] only by elimination—my volition is involved with and, so to speak, encased within a noetic act.

Let us say it again: consciousness always [means] a reference to objects [whether the modality in question is] willing, feeling, or thinking.

[Let us distinguish between] a noetic act and a performance, such as willing, desiring, or preferring. [Let us differentiate, say, between] taking notice and desiring.

The manner [we choose] to describe the noetic relationship [is of] the greatest importance. [Just compare] the ancient [concept of] *homoiosis* [likeness] and the modern [notion of] "content": the world is my repr[esentation]; *esse* [*est*] *percipi* [being consists in being perceived].[1]

The sphere of noetic acts [is] manifold. [We have various kinds of noetic act, such as]: [1] the presentative, exemplified by perceiving, imagining, and bringing to mind; [2] the connective, exemplified by distinguishing, relating, and deducing. . . . Neither sort is true or false.

[3] Judgment: [it is] the thesis involved in believing, holding a conviction, or making an assertion. [In this matter] the questions concerning subject and predicate are [entirely] secondary. Predication as affirmation: affirmation [is not to

be seen as] opposed to denial, but [only] to mere presentation. A sentence and the act of asserting a sentence.

[4] Question and answer.

What happens to the object which is first presented and then believed in? Or equivalently stated: What is the correlate of believing and affirming?

The world of objects vs. the world of *being*. The *steadfastness* of the object, or its performance value (*ejecutividad*).

The shadow (object) vs. the thing. Herein lies the meaning of the copula and the reason why *A* cannot be believed in. [We can believe only in the fact that] some *A* is.

The term "existence" is infected with the sense "reality," and yet relational qualities and, generally speaking, all ideal objects are endowed with the "existence" attributable to "being."

The manner in which belief casts its correlate out of the subject himself.

Truth and falsity [*pertain*] *only* [*to*] *an act of asserting a sentence or of believing.*

By virtue of a belief, the noetic act is a cognition.

The difficulties we experience in attempting to describe "being" have led some to see in value the correlate of belief.

Consciousness must employ a dual act or modality in order to be able to refer to a twofold value. To appraise a value negatively is tantamount to transforming it into a disvalue. There is no such thing as negative believing.

There is no act of non-believing which could be construed as an act of believing. Doubting is not the negation of believing. Comedy and tragedy.

The vacillation of consciousness consists in [living by] a belief which is dual and antithetical. I can doubt only if I believe that *A* is *B* and also that *A* is not *D* [*B*?].

Doubt resides within certainty, just as the insect's larva dwells in the very heart of the fruit. Doubt lives off certainty; if not, it would starve to death. Psychologically speaking, therefore, we can say that it is altogether impossible to consider doubt as one of the basic attitudes we may adopt. Doubt, regarded per se, is a secondary matter.

Doubt is the single combat between two [conflicting] beliefs. A and B attempt to avail themselves of a third belief, C, which [eventually] forms an alliance with one of them. Thereafter, the belief associated with C is believed in not by virtue of itself, but by reason of C. Here we have encountered the founded belief, or belief *because of*. . . . The foundation originates in doubt. Doubt is always a matter of foundations. Strictly speaking, there is no such thing as a definite, specific doubt which could be characterized as naïve. A blind or naïve belief results form the event by which a state of conviction becomes attached or stuck to a noetic thought or act.

10

The sciences presuppose the existence of truth. The mission of philosophy. Philosophy and skepticism. The conflict between truths. The principle involved here is devoid of sense.

EVERY THEORY is a system of truths.

Every truth must be confirmed, both universally and particularly. [Take,] for instance, a law—and science as a whole.

The sciences, without exception, rest on the monumental assumption that truth exists.

Like a gold thread, the idea of truth encircles, encloses, and holds in an entire cultural area. There are those who—in some corner or other within that realm—are solicitously at work, without harboring even the slightest suspicion that perhaps there is no truth at all, that the beehive is mere illusion. Now, think of the consequences should that prove to be the case, i.e., were truth in fact not to exist at all. The nonexistence of truth would transform scientific activity into a senseless, fictive, and empty exercise, since every science or part of a science is fundamentally based in the belief that we are in possession of a series of truths.

For science to be meaningful, truth must be ascertained and its grounds determined. And here lies precisely the first mission of philosophy: to provide unshakable foundations for the assumption out of which an entire cultural area is begotten.

Now the same is true in the domain of morality. There

we find that acts are approved or condemned on the basis of value judgments, which are taken as the means to distinguish good and evil. But what if the judgment by which we believe ourselves able to tell good from evil turns out to be a fiction? Here we have another entire cultural area built on an assumption: that the good exists, that there is such a thing as the value we term "goodness."

[And what about] beauty? If we carefully analyze the meaning we attach to the word "beautiful," we soon discover that assigning this qualification to some work [of art] amounts to bestowing supra-individual worth on it. Here the question involved does not pertain to the mere fact that I like the work of art. Rather we come face to face with the claim that I like it, because it is "objectively perfect."

For as long as we live, we sail aboard these presuppositions, i.e., we use them or put them into practice. Any attempt to identify their ground is then tantamount to bringing them to a state of crisis. In other words, any such venture would be equivalent to distancing ourselves from the spontaneous life of consciousness and to being translated to a sort of virtual life or life beyond the pale. But philosophy, the science of culture, or the science of the meaning of conscious life, [teaches that] *ho* [*de*] *anexétastos bíos ou bíotos anthrópos* [for man an unexamined life is not worth living].[1] This is the reason why philosophizing and living are at opposite poles.

[Or as] Fichte [put it]: "Both living and theorizing can only be determined in terms of one another. Strictly speaking, living is not philosophizing, and philosophizing is not living."[2]

We have already seen that the way philosophy operates, its method, must be different from the procedures followed in the other sciences, since the subject of first philosophy, the foundation of philosophy, is truth itself. In particular, philosophy ought to proceed without a basis in presuppositions, and especially without the assumption that truth exists.

But then how are we to proceed? If everything must ultimately be brought back to the problem of the existence of truth, to what shall we have recourse in order to resolve it?

We shall see what is needed to answer this question, at the right opportunity.

Doubtless we have to deal forthrightly with the case of absolute skepticism. But this is not a misfortune, nor even an irksome, irritating venture which has unexpectedly become our lot. Skepticism is no mere episodic occurrence in the career of philosophy, nor is the skeptic like a highwayman who suddenly happens upon the philosopher moving along the road and robs him. (In fact, the situation is just the reverse. As Herbart [thought], philosophy must start at the point of skepticism, just as surely as the sword begins at its pointed end.)

The skeptic was regarded only as a fact of existence by ancient philosophers, who, as I have pointed out, had not yet abandoned the natural style of thinking proper to prescientific consciousness, that is to say, thinking based on unsuspected belief. Philosophy had to respond to the skeptical challenge simply because, as a matter of fact, there were skeptical men.

Now then, that this position is way off the mark can be appreciated by recognizing that there have been no absolute skeptics. (Gorgias of Leontini). Indeed, skepticism is not philosophy at all, but rather an objection raised against the possibility of philosophy as such. In other words, skepticism is the [name for the] fundamental problem to be met by any philosophical system. If philosophy begins by doubting everything, the reason is not that it is in possession of definite reasons to do so. Rather it proceeds in that manner, because it is essentially a scientific endeavor devoid of any presuppositions.

This is the reason why philosophy becomes conscious of itself with Descartes. The [Cartesian] method consists in practicing methodical doubt, and it is not synonymous with the mere fact that we doubt. To doubt a proposition is the same as to demand proof of it: *lógon didonaí* [to render an account].[3] Only with proof does it become a true proposition, since, from believing that *A* is *B*, we pass into believing that "A is B" is true. We shall develop this point later.

We should not then have to wait for someone to come along and cast one or another proposition into doubt. We must from the very beginning enlarge the scope of our doubt to its greatest possible range; we must anticipate the full compass of the doubt, so as not to make use of anything which is or may be comprised thereby. That is why Descartes gave one of his "meditations" the title *De ce qu'on peut revoquer en doute* [Of the things which may be brought within the sphere of the doubtful], and not *De ce qu'on a revoqué en doute* [Of the things which have been brought within the sphere of the doubtful].[4]

Just as in Beethoven's sonata, "to joy by way of sorrow," so we have to come to the truth by means of doubt and reach philosophy through skepticism.

But the tools to practice doubt were already forged by the Greeks. In scientific endeavors, we have not yet exhausted the riches contained within the horizon established by Greek vision. We still see the same mountain ranges, the same horizon, the same trees.

Agrippa's five tropes continue to be efficacious, each according to its own measure. They are still the five ways effective in charging against truth. The first one is this: *ton apo tes diaphonías ton doxon*, or the argument on the basis of the discrepancy of opinion.[5] If we inspect our surroundings and, above all, if we look into the past, we find that the most conflicting opinions are being or have been advocated. Here we encounter the argument with the greatest practical impact. And this is even truer today than it was at the time of the Greeks.

History is a long-enduring horizon on which we witness the appearance of successive truths, in such a way that one truth is a stand against the other. Men have defended and still defend as true propositions which contradict one another. Can we possibly hope not to be subject to the same fate? Our own truth appears to us as one among many, as another factor contributing to the universal dissonance of opinion, particularly because during the last century we learned how to look at the past and understand it. We have come to realize that each historical period, in the last analysis, consists of a few tendencies and a few blind spots, within the confines of which individual men live. Every new century exhibits its own new enthusiasms and virtues, but it also comes on stage pierced by the arrow which will eventually strike it down. We have also learned how to place ourselves in the shoes of the men of each period; we have learned how to look at the world with the eyes of our predecessors and thus to find meaning in the body of their ideas and a justification for them. Accordingly, we have to see human life, on the one hand, as relative to its own times and, on the other, as a way of being which has its own justification. We no longer fall prey to the error typical of the eighteenth century, the error which was its very limitation, namely, the illusion that it could step out of the sequence of centuries and establish itself as the crowning age. We acknowledge that our own time is as much a link in an infinite chain as any other period. In fact, we succeed at transforming our own time into the past, into something impermanent and fleeting, by anticipating our future. And in this fashion we learn to regard ourselves with a mixture of pity and scorn, precisely the combination which constitutes the "historical sense."

([This is] certainly a genuinely democratic interpretation of history, since by virtue of it we have transformed our own day or century into no more than one among many, as Scheherazade used to say at the beginning of every one of her stories.)

And this too is the conclusion at which Agrippa arrived by following his own path, namely, that it is not possible for us ever to think the truth, since men believe in conflicting or differing views.

[This argument has] an assured emotional impact. But what about its theoretical value? Does it prove that truth does not exist? In fact, the argument is devoid of sense.

Why does this contention seem to prove that truth is impossible? The availability of a multiplicity of opinions is indeed no basis to raise any objection against the existence of truth. Consider this situation from the opposite side. The availability of such a multiplicity could lead you to make certain discoveries, provided that you are sincerely inclined to listen to the soft whispers born in the innermost recesses of the heart. For is it not there that you would locate the restlessness given expression in this argument? I mean the fact that you do not really have courage enough to assign paramount and final significance to your very own ideas, in opposition to the rest of mankind's. (This lack of self-confidence was at one point characteristic of our age. In fact, it was the reason why a time came when the crown of thought seemed to have been achieved by writers who fondled and nourished our distrust, vacillation, and bloodlessness by means of mere rhetorical argumentation. Take for instance Anatole France's *The Garden of Epicurus*: a work typical of its time, it does not contain a single, solitary idea which is clear and far-reaching. The book is no more than a voluptuary's encomium of our spiritual weakness.)

In other words, if there were no multiplicity of opinions, there would be no reason to cast doubt on the existence of truth. Then our criterion for truth would be the *consensus omnium*, or universal suffrage.

But really disagreement does not even establish the existence of error. Why can't all these different opinions be true in some sense or other? The reason is this: two contradictory opinions cannot both be true. Accordingly, if we find contradictory opinions, we have also discovered the existence of error. This discovery is a truth which evidently withstands any form of skeptical onslaught. It is that truth which allows us to recognize error in contradiction.

If we are to make of *diaphonía* [disagreement] the origin of doubt, we must first entertain absolutely no doubts about the nature of truth. Since truth is one, error would consist in the existence of a multiplicity of opinions. [Here we encounter] error as a special problem: How are such errors possible? Are they errors at all? History.

The [argument of] *ton pros ti*, or relativity.[6]

Knowledge is always born in and dies with an [individual, or] subject. It is without exception a subjective affair, including the case in which someone tells the true from the false. [Consider] Protagoras's view, to wit: that the true is whatever seems to be so to someone *(phaínesthai)*.[7] [Or take the case] of the [barber's] basin.[8]

Perhaps this is necessarily the case. If so, skepticism will find its origin in the very essence of knowledge. The passage from being to knowledge is mediated by the subject's intervention; knowledge and all its determinations derive from the nature of the given subject: tell me who you are and I will tell you what you think.

Truth is the feeling of evidence. [Let me refer you to the following:] belief, [William] James, and the emotional reaction of the whole man; [David] Hume's "customary connection";[9] [Friedrich] Nietzsche's view that the truth "*is that sort of error* without which a particular species cannot live."[10] The will-to-power: truths and values are coins minted in the die of great men's wills. Truth is a human affair, an all-too-human affair indeed. That something is true is identical with its seeming so to someone. Accordingly, the word "truth" expresses a relative *quid*, just as "large" and "small" do. We are changeable, and we wish to judge about what is changing. To each subject a different truth. Isis's disciple.

For [Georg] Simmel, philosophical truth [is] like art, like the dance. Truth is the originary dance of the soul, the modulation and rhythm thereof.

The primordial truths are the ways of bringing about or constituting something. To every subject a different truth.

[Theodor] Lipps, [John Stuart] Mill. The natural laws of thought. Psychologism. Lipps: knowledge as a biological activity. The principle of the economy of thought or [the axiom] of the least effort. This is the intellectual tendency of our times. Subjectivism, or subjectivistic relativism.

Is it true, then, that the sphere of the doubtful is boundless? Absolute skepticism. [According to] Kant, such is not an opinion to be taken seriously. Things as parts of a series.

11

Two of Agrippa's tropes. Psychologism. Subjectivism. Sense[, non-sense, and counter-sense].

IN THE PRECEDING LECTURE, we began forming an acquaintance with two of Agrippa's tropes, which are the enduring sources of skepticism. I mean, first of all, the argument based on the discrepancy of opinion (i.e., *ton apo tes diaphonías*). Second, I am referring to the argument based on the relativity of truth with regard to a given individual, or subject (i.e., *ton pros ti*): inasmuch as the activity of cognition is always the subject's own, there is no real, but only seeming truth.

On that occasion, I pointed out that the first argument is devoid of any theoretical impact, and yet, emotionally speaking, wins our hearts. Now then, the fact that we regard the discrepancy of opinion as a sign that we cannot know the truth precisely takes for granted our possession of the genuine concept of truth. In other words, such a recognition presupposes that we know the nature of truth. In this argument, we may say that we regard the existence of a multiplicity of conflicting opinions as flying in the face of the truth, but this is the result of taking all such opinions as true, while [implicitly] acknowledging that truth is necessarily one. It is then possible to identify in this position a desire to have all men think the same [thought] about the same thing, a sort of fear of finding ourselves completely alone, while engaged in the defense of what we believe to be true against the opposition of many. This is an urge to extend the principle of the *volonté générale* [general will], which rules in a democracy, to the sphere of logic. But what is valid in a democracy is invalid in logic, so those who harbor a deep love for democracy would do well not to play the democrat's part out of place. We can never infer the nonexistence of truth on the grounds of the discrepancy of opinion. In fact, the valid inference would proceed precisely in the opposite direction. The special question concerning the possibility of the discrepancy of opinion may be raised only on the basis of the available evidence concerning the nature of truth. It makes sense to wonder about the multiplicity of truths only because we think we know that truth is one.

On the other hand, the power of conviction connected with the trope of relativity continues to exercise its influence unabatedly and decisively. The subject leads his life always within the confines of his own self; as the Arabic proverb puts it, he cannot step out of his own shadow. Within our own selves, truth presents itself as the accent we place on the most different and even opposite matters. How are we to distinguish the accent we give to the right conviction from that we place on the erroneous one? We are bereft of any external guidance; we lack the transcendent teacher who would keep our path straight. We are alone, all alone within our very selves, so much so that anything whatever must first become our own flesh, so to speak, if it is to gain access to our inner realm. From one belief of ours we have recourse to another, and without ever breaking the circle, we make our dream of yesterday the judge of our dream of today. Abiding alone, how shall we ever be able to tell the true from the false in a region lying always beyond ourselves? In the *Theaetetus*, Plato speaks of the [sphere of] truths and errors as an aviary, wherein a blindfolded man strives to capture only doves amidst a flock of doves and pigeons.[1]

This trope is harsh indeed; it seems to be a sentence

beyond appeal. Having taken a quick glance at its history, we have learned how it adopted various forms and—especially during the second half of the nineteenth century—exercised the greatest influence and became the governing principle of European consciousness.

Subjectivism is the style of thinking characteristic of our times. As I have already pointed out, it is not a new position or truth which we strive on our own to reach. On the contrary, it is the prejudice and the tradition which form the basis of our departures. We shall deal with subjectivism in some detail, and I have already prepared the way by pointing out that it adopts two basic forms, psychologism and biologism. The reasoning is the same in both, although the latter goes somewhat further than the former.

Both positions contend that only those intellectual acts which obey certain fundamental laws may be called true. Such are the laws of thought or logic. Take for instance a thought harboring within itself a contradiction: such a mental event is false because it violates the law of thought which proscribes contradiction. In the final analysis, the examination of any specific thought as to truth or falsity will have recourse to the principles of identity and noncontradiction. On the basis of such axioms we derive the determinations of truth and falsity which we make about all our propositions. As long as we move in the sphere of the latter, both of us—those who adopt the subjectivistic position in logical questions and those who, like me, espouse an absolutistic stance—proceed along a common road. But the moment we inquire into the nature of the laws themselves, we find the subjectivist contending that they are laws precisely in the same sense in which universal gravitation is a law governing the behavior of bodies. In his view, accordingly, the factual make-up of our thought would never permit us to incur contradiction; so to speak, our thought would not assimilate contradiction.

Few and far between are the books published in the second half of the nineteenth century which are not based on this opinion, whatever version of it they may use or whatever mitigating qualifications they may add. Take [John] Stuart Mill [for instance]. As the representative man [of his period], he tells us that such laws are "inherent necessities of thought," "an original part of our mental constitution," [and] "laws of our thoughts by the native structure of the mind."[2]

Strictly speaking and taking the term in its pregnant sense, we can say that *psychologism* is the name for this position, since it contends that the laws of logic or the laws of truth are constitutive, i.e., that they are psychological laws or principles which constitute the make-up of the thinking subject. In our case, the laws of logic would be necessary constituents of the human intellect, of the psychological species "man." *Biologism* would only take the further step of reducing the mental sphere to the level of organic function and of regarding the so-called laws of the intellect—together with the laws of heredity and evolution—as results of the general biological principle according to which an organism employs the shortest and most direct pathways for its own preservation.

Left to its own devices, a muscle extends and contracts according to its own law or physiological necessity, whence derives a rhythmical motion which constitutes the natural play or dance of the muscle. In the same way, logic or truth would be the natural play or dance of the soul, its own modulation and rhythm.

As you can see, the notion of the spirit of the times or of epochal consciousness is no conceptual illusion. Words like those we have just used provoke our spontaneous allegiance; even those among you who have never philosophized must have found them clear, illuminating, and true. By contrast, they would have impressed a [classical] Greek as absurdities, or at least as paradoxes. To think that things are what they are, not because they are so constituted, but because our subjective make-up dictates it, would have made him giddy, just as those were made giddy who heard for the first time that the earth turns about the sun, with us following in its retinue, like stones after their slings.

In this regard, [Theodor] Lipps has limited himself to recasting the profession of faith of his own times by means of luminious formulae. He has not even failed to refer to those disquieting entities known as "things-in-themselves." Taken to be exactly the opposite of what Leibniz and Kant thought, such items have been the philosophical bric-a-brac used as standard decoration in every intellectual barbershop in Europe for the last hundred years. It goes without saying, of course, that Lipps—one of the keenest and most truthful intellects of our times—has never ceased to correct his utterances of 1880 and to convey his sorrow over them. In fact, he has been among the first to engage in a collaborative effort to cure the collective aberration which the faith expressed by such words makes manifest.

But let us return to our reading of the relevant passages. Lipps said:

. . . We think correctly, in the material sense, when we think of things as they are. But for us to say, certainly and indubitably, that things are like this or like that, means that the nature of our mind prevents us from thinking of them otherwise. For one need not repeat what has been so often uttered, that one can obviously not think of a thing as it is, without regard to the way in which one must think of it, nor can one make of it so isolated an object of knowledge. The man, therefore, who compares his thought of things with the things themselves can in fact only measure his contingent thinking, influenced by custom, tradition, inclination and aversion, against a thinking that is free from such influences, and that heeds no voice but that of its own inherent lawfulness.

The rules, therefore, on which one must proceed in order to think rightly are merely rules on which one must proceed in order to think as the nature of thought, its specific lawfulness, demands. They are, in short, identical with the natural laws of thinking itself. Logic is a physics of thinking or it is nothing at all.[3]

Concerning this understanding and characterization of the laws of thought, we come to a parting of the ways. As long as we are engaged—to express it as we did before—in the analysis of one or another particular truth, we do not notice any discrepancy, but now, since we are focusing our attention on the meaning of the very principles which constitute truth itself, we realize that every particular truth exhibits one coloring for the subjectivist and another for the non-subjectivist.

And this forces us to formulate our problem so as to do justice to its full range. But in order to do so, and to endow it with the greatest possible clarity, let us state the question as a theorem.

I shall characterize as subjectivistic (or relativistic) any theory of knowledge wherein truth is understood to be dependent—in one fashion or another—on the make-up of the cognitive subject. I am referring therefore to any theory according to which it can be asserted that what is true for one subject may not be so for another. (I mean, for example, a position which holds that what is true for man may not be true for the inhabitant of the star Sirius, or for an angel, or for God.)

On the basis of this nominal definition, I shall first of all affirm that any kind of subjectivism (or relativism) is a form of skepticism. Second, I shall say that the proposition at the root of skepticism is an absurdity.

As you can see, the second point is decisive. For this reason, and to avoid unnecessary repetition, I shall begin my analysis by considering the second thesis.

The ideal proposition on which skepticism rests is this: there is no truth; we possess none.

What could possibly be the attitude for science to adopt when confronted with an assertion of this kind? Are ways open to science to annihilate it? Or should science just ignore it, leaving it out of consideration as if it were an uncivil and extravagant person? May science begin with a profession of faith? As we saw in one of the preceding lectures, faith is a blind form of science, one which believes on the basis of no reason at all. It is not the other way around; [that is to say, faith does not believe something][4] because it is proven to be true. On another occasion, we shall pause long enough to describe with some care the psychological difference between faith and knowledge, but today it is not convenient to entangle ourselves in that suggestive topic. Moreover, even to attempt to do so would require that we determine first what—I hope—we shall find out today. We need to keep in view the fact that in science we strive to believe on the basis of grounds and proofs. And it goes without saying that grounds and proofs exist in the world only because doubt itself is possible. Truth needs grounds in order to buttress itself against the onslaught of doubt. This fact, and this fact only, the finding of a secure defense against the siege of doubt, is responsible for the difference between [scientific] truth and faith.

For these reasons, the death knell would sound for science if it were forced to keep inimical, heavy-laden doubt wandering about outside its walls. Some have simply assumed that science must take notice only of a well-founded doubt.

[Accordingly,] a proposition such as the one at the root of skepticism, which does not even claim to prove itself, would be entirely harmless. And yet this is not so. It makes no sense whatever to require skepticism to become science and truth, inasmuch as skepticism means the denial of [the possibility of] science and the refusal of the [existence of] truth.

But are we not then defenseless? Have we not therefore surrendered? How would it be possible to show that truth in fact exists in knowledge to someone who is ready to deny the very presuppositions of any proof whatever? Is it perchance true that science stands on feet of clay, like the biblical colossus?

There is only one possible way out: to find some truth so privileged that it would be the foundation of itself. Such a truth would make absurd the effort of anyone to deny it.

Perhaps this is the situation involving the skeptic's thesis. As you remember, I pointed out that posing the problem of whether or not we in fact possess the truth was impossible unless we first raised the prior question concerning the nature of truth itself. How could we ever come to know whether or not we have something, or whether or not we may in fact see it, without first coming to know what it is? But if this is so, the question itself—the very doubt concerning the possibility of our having the truth—is meaningful, provided we first assert that we already are in possession of one truth, namely, the genuine notion of the truth. Only if we know what knowledge is does it become intelligible to say that we know nothing.

To deny we have the capacity to possess the truth presupposes that we know the conditions under which such possession could take place. But how could someone identify these conditions without, at the same time, allowing himself to share in them? Now this means that the way to handle the skeptic's thesis is not to confront it with reasons external to itself, but rather to confront it with itself. Unless this thesis dies by its own hand, we cannot expect anyone or anything ever to give life to the truth.

I have just spoken of the situation metaphorically, referring to the death or suicide of a proposition. We should now ask about its real nature, about what it is without any metaphor. Simply put, the situation is as follows: the proposition is self-contradictory, since it says both what it [obviously] means and the opposite as well.

A skeptic might retort that all of that is well and good, but is also immaterial to his thesis. And the reason is this: only those who believe in the existence of truth find in self-contradiction the equivalent of a death knell; if a truth exists in fact, it would at least exclude contradiction, but he who does not accept the existence of the truth does not accept the truth of the principle of noncontradiction either. (Klopstock's *Odes*.) The same reasoning applies against the common argument raised time and again in opposition to the skeptics. The skeptics say: There is no truth. And the reply is forthcoming: You have incurred contradiction, for, in saying there is no truth, you are claiming that what you are saying is true, or, if you do not make any such claim, then it is evident that you yourselves acknowledge that your contention is not true. To this argument, the skeptics have replied since the time of Aenesidemus that in fact they make no claim to speak the truth. They claim only that they do not know whether there is truth, that truth seems to them not to exist. They do not judge; rather they practice the *epokhé*, the act of refraining or holding back from judging.

As you can see, the duel is to the death, and the skeptic is seemingly reborn out of his own ashes.

The fact that [the proposition][5] in question is self-contradictory does not entail that it is not true. Self-contradiction does not annul the truth value of the proposition; rather it annihilates the proposition *qua* proposition.

Truth, falsehood, and doubt are not primary facts. The world[s] of the true, the false, and the doubtful are just provinces of a realm which both transcends and encompasses them. All truths are living parts of the truth, but truth itself lives in a climate and is built of a material to which truth and falsity are irrelevant. The fact that the conflicts so identified do really occur points in the direction of some support, beyond the truth, on which we would have to stand.

Now let us simply and plainly consider what I believe to be the first great discovery proper to the twentieth century.[6] Almost all of you are presently going to hear for the first time about something which will become a new commonplace in the next few years.

What I am talking about could not be more ordinary or trivial, for nothing is more banal than saying that a phrase is meaningful or that it is not.

Mind you, I am not saying that it is either true or false. I ask: What is that we call "sense," which utterances either have or do not have?

Consider the following: "Now we are not in Madrid." We can say that this statement is not true, precisely because it is endowed with sense. [Now] take the following: "and but no." About it I cannot even say that it is not true, since this combination of words is entirely devoid of sense.

[Again consider the following:] "a round square." [We can say that] it is false to assert that such a thing exists. In this case, I am not affirming anything. The expression in question is endowed with sense, but its sense is an impossible one.

[Accordingly, we may distinguish among three different cases:] the false, the non-sensical, and the absurd, or countersensical.

Please note, then, that before anything may be true, false, or doubtful, it must be endowed with sense and free from absurdity. It is then in [the domain of] sense that counter-sense, or absurdity, is constituted for automatic self-destruction. We must understand a proposition before we can accept or reject it. And *sense* is the object of the act of understanding.

What subtle material does sense consist of? It is not even visible, and yet it is the most indestructible of things. While iron and diamond are subject to corruption, the sense something has escapes its clutches.

[Consider] Plato's Ideas.

At every moment, we are participating in those "natures."

Take a perception. I can describe what I am seeing, and whatever I am able to communicate to you would be part and parcel of the sense of my visual experience. *That which* I am seeing will perish; I will perish too, but the sense of my visual experience is everlasting.

[Here we have distinguished three things:] the object, the *act*, and the sense [of the act]. [The sense of the act] is immutable and certain. We may be undergoing a halluci-nation, but the *sense* of the hallucination is never halluci-natory.

On the one hand, *sense* is free of the difficulties and perils to which things or being are subject. On the other hand, sense is as free of subjective admixture as being is.

[Let us remind ourselves of] Descartes's [hypothesis of the] evil genius. Such a being is singularly incapable of making me disbelieve that I am seeing what I am seeing, say, that color *A* and color *B* are . . . the same color. The evil genius is unable to make me fail to understand what I am in fact understanding.

This will suffice.

Now let us examine the sense of the skeptic's thesis, while setting aside the question of whether or not it is true.

What do we understand by truth? Everything depends on answering this question.

12

Skepticism. Sense, identity, and counter-sense.
Relativism today. *Quid est veritas?* Belief. The
possibility of truth. Relativism and truth.

AS YOU MAY APPRECIATE, no problem can ever be resolved
as long as our understanding of it is only incompletely clarified. And if this is true in general, it is even more so for
the problem raised by skepticism, which is the problem par
excellence. Every problem is tantamount to a demand for
greater clarity; in fact, it is our hope for plain daylight in
the land of sunset. There is no use, then, in moving about
the skeptic's thesis by uttering vague generalities concerning
the sorrowful experience of error which has been man's
throughout history. For our purposes here, lamentations are
as ineffectual as wild enthusiasms. Philosophical skepticism
is not a form of melancholy; it is not a sorrow beyond
definition or an unfocused uneasiness let loose within our
breast. If it were, no one could ever be cured of the ailment,
except those who found relief in the unctuous effusions of
mystical preaching.

The question at hand is entirely theoretical. But "theory"
[literally] means "vision," and vision is a striving after clarity. He who lacks the daring will to see clearly, he who
does not possess such a tragic and Luciferian will, should
never speak of truth or doubt, because it is in such experiences that culture makes its first beginnings. As Goethe
has suggested, culture is—first of all, above all, and after

all—a great urge to move from darkness to clarity, an indomitable will to see in plain daylight.

I say this because I know we are often intimidated by the shadow which words cast in mid-air, a shadow which prevents us from moving straightforwardly to grasp their concrete meaning. Owing to the resulting imprecision, words come to have magical power over us, an influence which, strictly speaking, has nothing to do with them.

Accordingly, in confronting the skeptic's thesis, our task is only to pay heed to what it says and to examine its meaning. We shall discharge our obligation if we make clear that the thesis does in fact destroy itself. It is not necessary to establish the opposite thesis in order to show that skepticism is an unacceptable position. In other words, we are not required first to develop a sound theory concerning the nature of truth and of our possession of it.

In previous lectures, I have said that skepticism—although itself impossible as a theory—finds its justification in being an objection raised against the very possibility of theory. Like Mephistopheles, skepticism brings about good by willing evil, for by endlessly attempting to deny all, it forces us to affirm and secure everything on a sound basis. Evidence for this is the fact that we have stumbled upon a richer, firmer, and clearer world than the worlds of being and truth. And we have come to this discovery under the pressures of the demands of skepticism, which imposed the need for some privileged instance upon which no doubt at all could be cast. It may very well be that things are not as they seem truly to be for us. It may even be that Descartes was right in fearing—as he in fact did in carrying his attitude of mistrust to the limit—that there exists an evil genius, who takes pleasure in manipulating our thoughts so as to deceive us always. And yet, even so, it will not come to pass that we think B when we are actually thinking A; it will never happen that the sense we are grasping is not what we are in fact grasping.

As I have said, the true, the false, and the doubtful must be endowed with sense before they may be considered true, false, or doubtful. If there is no sense to the utterance, neither will there be truth, falsity, or doubt.

The only thing a skeptic cannot give up is this: that his words have sense. Soon we shall attempt to inquire into the nature of "sense." An investigation of that sort—which I have called noology—constitutes, I believe, the foundation of everything else, being a priori for logic, psychology, mathematics, and metaphysics. At this point, we need only understand this truism: if we are to be able to cast doubt on something, the thing doubted must be itself and not something else which we are not doubting.

Accordingly, we have to dwell no longer on the skeptic's self-destructive proposition, for he who says "There is no truth" or "I doubt we possess the truth," or who uses any other equivalent expression, is actually thinking the truth and distinguishing it from falsity. In fact, the skeptic does not allow for the "possibility" that the two have one and the same sense. The validity of the principle of identity is a condition to be met, if doubting is to be a process endowed with sense. I cannot cast doubts on my doubting, if that which I am doubting is not self-identical and different from everything else. This is the reason why the skeptic's proposition is as much counter-sense as a round square. We can never succeed in thinking it through; and this realization will do for our purposes. We do not strive for any certitude about our cognitions and opinions which would be greater than this: denying or doubting them would imply a contradiction. As you may remember, our purpose was to anticipate the entire scope of possible doubt, in order to ensure that the contents of science could never be subject to doubt.

Now then, at this point our position can be formulated as follows: any possible doubt ceases the moment contradiction arises, since doubting must meet certain requirements without which it would not be itself. One such requirement is that the very sense of doubting presupposes the sense of many truths, among which we may cite the following: for one, that what we are thinking must remain self-identical; for another, that doubt should exist; also, that the doubter himself should exist, etc. Strictly speaking, to doubt will not be possible for us unless we believe in a realm containing literally an infinite number of truths.

The impossibility of denying the possibility of truth was referred to by [Rudolf H.] Lotze as the *Selbstvert[r]auen der Vernunft* [the self-confidence of reason] and by Jonas Cahan as the *Selbstgarantie der Wahrheit* [truth's self-warrant].

To engage as we have in the analysis of the thesis of absolute skepticism is necessary for construction of the ideal edifice of science. And yet to do so would be uninteresting, as I am sure you understand, were it not for the fact that we must test all historically established theories of truth—especially those which have currency today—against the results of the critique of absolute skepticism.

There is an error that exceeds every other, an absolute error which, if committed, would invalidate the theory in question to the highest degree. Such an error would consist in constructing a theory which would itself deny the very conditions making any theory possible. Since a "theory" is—first of all—an order and system of truths, it is evident that the negation of truth, the denial of the very sense of truth, would render any theory impossible in principle. But an error of this sort is a formal constituent of the skeptic's position. This is why I have sometime said that skepticism, or the denial of truth, is absolute error itself.

But now let us proceed to examine contemporary relativism, this being a more fruitful and suggestive task indeed. Relativism is a position taken about truth. In fact, it means to be nothing but the theory of truth, or the truth about truth. As I have pointed out on other occasions, adopting the thesis of relativism is tantamount to affirming that truth is relative to the cognitive subject. Let us now ask whether or not such an assertion is identical with absolute skepticism, the contention which denies the very sense of truth.

It is high time for us to ask ourselves the question once put to the just man of Galilee at the *praetorium* during a dramatic afternoon: *Quid est veritas?*[1]

What do we understand by "truth," the features of which we have been attempting to determine and the existence or nonexistence of which we have been inquiring into?

All that I have said so far in these lectures will now prove useful, and in fact will permit me to be brief in discharging the present task.

As I have said, things are neither true nor false. Only our consciousness or thought of things can be true or false. And then not every kind of thought can be so characterized. The image I may entertain of a chimera is neither true nor false, and neither is a hallucinatory perception. If I were suddenly to see not this room filled by a gracious public, but one transformed into a dreadful jungle teeming with wild beasts, there would be no doubt that I was in fact witnessing such a scene.

(Truth and falsity make their presence felt the moment I proceed from representing, imagining, or perceiving something to judging or believing it.

As Kant says, "the senses do not err—not because they always judge rightly but because they do not judge at all."[2]

On the other hand, Heraclitus says, "Witnesses, but not bad judges.")

Our analysis of judging has led us to determining that

belief is the essential component thereof, for to judge that
A is B is to believe that, in fact, A is B. But what is the
meaning of "in fact"?

In order to grasp this point clearly, we must refer briefly
to the recent investigations of the Austrian thinker A[lexius]
Meinong. I specifically have in mind what he calls *Annahmen*, or assumptions. In logic, judging was traditionally defined as the act by which we affirm or deny; such a duality
was taken as characteristic of the act of judging. In imagining, we actually neither affirm nor deny anything; in perceiving, it is doubtful whether we are affirming something,
but it is evident that we are not denying and could not ever
deny anything. And yet Meinong has underscored a commonplace, which we continually put to good use in our
habitual mental conduct. Just note the difference between
saying "War is an act of barbarism" without qualifications
of any kind and asserting "That war is an act of barbarism
seems highly doubtful to me." The first utterance appears
as a component in the second, and yet does not seem to
have the same meaning. If I say of the component in question that its content is doubtful, how can I be taken to have
affirmed it in the totality in which it functions as an element?
I have judiciously refrained from doing so, for has the utterance not lost something in its second use (as compared
with its meaning in its first use)? In the first use, I assigned
to my words, so to speak, a performance value, which in
the second use, I did not employ, since I did not assert
therein that war is an act of barbarism.

There is another instance of this sort of meaning change,
the significance of which may be easier to grasp. I am referring to what happens to an expression when we place the
conditional operator "if" before it. Suppose that at this point
I were to say, "The lights are off now." You would certainly
take my assertion as false. But suppose instead that I had
said, "If the lights are off now, we are in the dark." In this

case, you would regard my contention as quite credible. The first utterance is an instance of judgment proper; the second is an example of what Meinong called an assumption. Both have the same objective content, open in each to being asserted or denied, and yet the assumption lacks the performance or assertive value, the sort of fundamental efficacy characteristic of judgment. In the final analysis, we would have to say that an assumption is the shadow of a judgment, the gap for a missing judgment, a neutralized, impaired judgment. And, as we well know, the advantage of the judgment over the assumption is the presence of belief, the thesis proper to conviction.

I am not sure whether you consider these distinctions just matters of detail. In my view, anything worth anything— say, a Gobelin tapestry, a poem, a science, or a friendship— is but a tissue of details and humble threads. Reality is nothing other than the infinite sum of small things. And this is so much so that, should God have made little of detail upon creating reality, I believe He would not have brought about the world but would have just delivered a speech. The thinker ought to be loyal to the small, just as the Creator is.[3]

All right; let us now turn to belief.

We believe not in things, but in our thinking of them. A thought or mental performance accompanied by belief is modified by the claim that something which is not the mind itself, or which transcends consciousness, corresponds to the mental event. In short: to believe is to believe that a being corresponds to our consciousness.

"Being": this is a terrible word indeed, the terrible word proper to metaphysics, a word bristling with ambiguities, a word which, like Medusa's head, we do not know how to seize.

For our purposes, however, it will suffice to point out that *being* is that capacity which turns things into things or reality into reality, and by virtue of which things and reality do not depend on subjectivity or consist in being mere fictions.

When I feign something, I do not take it as if it existed; I do not regard it as available beyond the sphere of my feigning. What I make believe is not real; the only real thing about it is the act by which I feign it. The act of feigning begins at one point and ends at another, and so does what I feign by means of it. Belief, by contrast, attests that what is believed in endures in itself, independently of my act of believing in it, and that, therefore, it neither arises nor perishes with the latter.

Let us not forget that we are only attempting to describe our believing *qua* phenomenon. At this point, we are not concerned with the question of whether or not the claim inherent in our belief is justified.

In this spirit, we may take all our beliefs to be so many illusions, if we wish. Nevertheless, a belief, as such, is always a claim that what we believe in is not an illusion, that it is the opposite of an illusion, that realities correspond to the objective contents of the belief, or that realities are reflected in them.

In short, believing is being conscious of something as *being*, as independent of my consciousness of it.

It is most difficult to render this point easily accessible. I would propose the following approach: as color is to seeing, so being is to believing; it is, so to speak, what believing sees. The eye sees color, but believing sees *being*, i.e., sees that color *is*.

Now then, only a belief, taken in this sense, can ever be true or false. Truth and falsity are qualities exhibited by beliefs.

Someone may wonder how this is possible. On the basis of what has been said, I would contend that every belief, even an illusory one, takes as *being* that which is thought.

[In this sense,] therefore, every belief takes itself to be true. How could there ever be a belief which would take itself as false?

Now let us proceed gradually, by steps. If anywhere, it is here, concerning the formidable question of truth, that we are obliged to make the most subtle distinctions. We are now engaged in securing and giving the final touch to that evanescent point on which the vast and sacred realm of culture has come to rest. In my opinion, there is no more suitable occasion to move cautiously and attentively.

As we shall see immediately, any superficiality and carelessness concerning these matters can only cause the gravest anomalies in the rest of the scientific edifice. We are here handling those truths which support the rest. And not only that: our very heart is engulfed by them; our science and art, our economy and law, our morality and God, will breathe in the atmosphere we are now preparing for them.

Let us proceed gradually. This is what I cautioned you about a moment ago. I have said that believing consists in taking as *being* that which is thought, but I have not contended at all that every belief holds itself to be true. [Let me explain the apparent contradiction.]

When I assert that A is B, I believe only that A is B. I do not thereby hold that two different things are both true, namely, "A is B" and "my belief that A is B." Isn't it apparent to you that the latter is another belief, inasmuch as its content is different? In belief α I hold there is a connection between A and B; in belief N I hold there is a connection between belief α and truth. Truth is a quality which I *believe* I have found in belief α.

Now the nature of such a quality is no longer a vexing matter to us.

If to believe is to hold that A is B, then such a belief will be true when the claim [inherent] therein is confirmed, that is to say, when in fact it is the case that A is B. In order to ascertain this, I have to compare belief α with the things themselves, i.e., with the very things we call A and B, and not with their concepts.

The belief that A is $B = N$

N is T (True)

I suspect this makes clear what we understand by truth: it is a quality acquired by a proposition or belief when we take its thought content as coincident with reality. Or in the words of the traditional formulation: *adaequatio intellectus et rei* [the adequate correspondence between the intellect and the thing (thought about by the intellect)].

Among the words we use, "knowledge" is one of those employed in the vaguest possible way, but it should signify only that belief by which we advert to the truth of another belief. To see something is not to know it. I know something only when I believe that the propositions I advance about it are true.

These definitions concerning the meaning of belief, truth, and knowledge have cost me dearly, and yet they are not brilliant insights, but mere truisms. If you have taken them down, I would highly appreciate it if you would try them for size when you are by yourselves, and if you would refine them and compare them to one another. It is remarkable that very few books are formally devoted to clarifying these fundamental *concepts*.

But you must have wondered how it is possible to hold

that the truth of a proposition consists in our having seen that it coincides with being itself, with the things themselves. If this condition had to be met, there would be no truth at all, for how could we ever compare our thoughts with the things themselves? We can never gain access to the latter, except by other acts of consciousness, [and to these by still other such acts,] and so on and so forth. We can never escape from ourselves, since subjectivity is governed by a most tragic principle, that of self-imprisonment. If being a perpetual prisoner is a terrible condition, how much more grim and horrible will the situation be of a prisoner who is his own jailer. [Friedrich?] Hebbel used to say that "it is impossible for a key to be locked away in the cabinet it is meant to unlock,"[4] and yet no more impossible is the opposite situation: having the subject step out of himself to take a look at being, precisely and exactly as it is.

This is, in fact, the conviction of the historical period which calls itself the Modern Age, and especially of the nineteenth century, its maximum embodiment. In all probability, I hold a different conviction. I am not "modern" at all, since I yearn to be a man of the twentieth century. And among other reasons, our century perhaps differs from the nineteenth in having no great desire either to be modern or to bring back the dead.

In any case, whether or not we think it possible to come into direct contact with the things themselves, the subject for our consideration today remains unaltered, for I have not at all attempted to show how truth is possible. I have limited myself to rendering the meaning of truth precise, to showing what it is we seek when we search after truth. So much the worse for ourselves, then, if later it turns out that the very structure of our minds makes us singularly inapt to secure it. However, I think it impermissible merely to engage in a so-called analysis of the cognitive means at our disposal, and thus to limit our search to that which such

cognitive means can indeed produce. An analysis of that
sort would disregard what our immediate sense of truth is,
for it would take the product of our cognitive operations—
no matter what it may be—as the meaning of truth itself.
Vain effort, indeed! Believing in such a quasi-truth would
amount to holding that whatever is affirmed by the belief
in question really *is*; the being, certainty, and necessity established in such a belief would not be open to reservations
or arguments. Whenever anyone believes that truth is relative, he believes it absolutely.

And yet someone may object that believing admits of
degrees, for I may believe something to be certain, or to be
possible, or to be more or less likely, and so on and so forth.
This is indeed true, but herein we can appreciate the curious
nature of believing: when I believe it probable that *A* is *B*,
I claim that such a probability is a certainty. When anyone
declares that something is probable, he is in fact declaring
that such a probability is absolutely the case. The calculus
of probabilities is not in turn a matter of probability, but
of certainty.

Now we can grasp that doubting itself amounts to effecting a modification in the general character proper to
believing. It is not the case that when I cast doubt on something, I entertain no belief about it; on the contrary, I believe—beyond the shadow of a doubt—that the thing is
doubtful. The doubtfulness appears to me with the firmness
of a certainty, but in such a way that the firmness encompasses the modality "doubtful." In other words, being probable, being questionable, or being doubtful are always manners of being, sharing in the latter by preserving its
immutability and solidity. [Edmund] Husserl[5]—to whom
we are so greatly indebted in all of these questions—points
out that it would be erroneous to consider doubting, opin-
ing, entertaining a suspicion, taking something as probable,
and so on as so many modalities of consciousness, among

which we could also find certain belief, or full, pure, and simple conviction. Such is not the case at all. To grasp his point, we need only pay careful attention to the meaning of such modalities. We will soon discover that they are connected by one essential vein, which gives them all life: certainty of belief is constantly present in each and every one of them, and thus constitutes itself as the originary modality of believing consciousness. Doubting, taking something as probable, and so on are, strictly speaking, modalities of belief, just as being healthy and being ill are modalities of being alive.

Perhaps you do not see this point today as clearly as I do. But no matter, for I hope it will be evident to you some time in the future.

Having finished our examination, we must do one more thing, if we are to make manifest the contradiction or absurdity at the heart of any theory propounding the *relativity* of truth, or proposing that the quality "truth" depends on the make-up of the subject. For this purpose, we only have to draw the consequences which immediately follow from our analyses.

Above all, let us keep in mind that when I believe that a proposition—say, "A is B"—is true, it may very well be that *A* is not really *B*. In this case, I am said to have committed an error; I have taken as true for me what, strictly speaking, is not true. Notice that I have used the word "true" in two different ways: first, by itself; second, in reference to me. At this juncture, it would be most useful for you to attempt to determine, with the utmost clarity, what you understand by "true for me," as well as the difference between that phrase and the simple expression "truth," or "truth in itself," to use the words of the great [Bernard] Bolzano.[6] You would soon realize that, after all is said and done, there is absolutely no difference. To say that something is true for me means that I believe that a given reality corresponds to my thought, and to say that something is true in itself, or just true, means that a given reality corresponds to my thought. Now suppose I have made a mistake. Then my proposition will no longer be true in itself, and, ceasing to be such, it will also cease to be true at all, that is to say, it will no longer even be true for me.

[We should not rest our case here, however.] When such difficult matters are before us, it is always useful to convey them in various ways, so that one expression will succeed with some, and a different one with others, in provoking the sudden illumination of understanding. Accordingly, another way of putting this point across would be to say that something is true for me when it is true in itself for me. Suppose I have committed an error. In that case, I have taken as true in itself what, strictly speaking, is no such thing. Upon realizing this, I will cease to regard as true in itself what strictly speaking has no such status, but the moment it is no longer true in itself, neither will it be true for me. As you see, everything revolves around an inevitable equivocation in the expression "true for me." First, we would have an asburd or impossible sense for the utterance in question, according to which we would seemingly refer to a kind of truth other than the truth which is in itself, or without qualifications. Second, we would have a different meaning for the same expression, namely, that the proposition "A is B" is true *for me*. In this case, the qualification "for me" does not affect the predicate "true," but only the connection—perhaps erroneously established by me—between "A is B," on the one hand, and "true," on the other. Let us say, for example, that "Oranges are blue" is an instance of what is true for me. In other words, that oranges are blue is for me absolutely true; in my view everyone is obliged to acknowledge that oranges are blue. Please notice the absurdity of the situation which would result if I were to assign to the expression "true for me" the first sense we identified. It would be tantamount to saying that oranges are not blue in fact, but are nevertheless blue for me. The notion "*being* for me" would then be like that of a round square or of a knife without blade or handle. But this is precisely the gist of Cervantes' divine, despairing jest when he makes Don Quixote, on being confronted with the barber's basin, finally arrive at the conclusion that ["what appears to you as a barber's basin appears to me as Mambrino's helmet, and to another it will appear as something else."][7] In other words, our situation is as follows: our opinions are various and conflicting, and we are all agreed about only one thing—that, to each of us, it does not appear that something just appears to be thus and so; rather, the thing appears to us to *be* precisely as it appears to us. The fact that there is error does not add or take away an iota from the "truth," which is our goal; it simply means that we believe we see truth where there is none. At night, when we fearfully walk paths teeming with possible and woeful dangers, we may believe we see a man where in fact there is just bramble. The error we have then committed lies precisely in believing that we saw a man, a genuine man. Likewise, when we commit a cognitive error, we in fact believe we have grasped a truth, one which is genuinely and absolutely so, where in fact [none][8] is available. If we did not take "man" to mean a real man, we would harbor no fears at all. If we were never really to regard as simply true anything we might think, then no occasion for error would ever arise.

For the time being, I do not think I can find a way of making this point clearer to you. In fact, only your reflection [could accomplish this.]

(A guideline: never confuse these two different questions. On the one hand, what is the meaning of truth? On the other hand, how is it possible for us ever to come to possess it?)

13

What is the meaning of truth? Relativism and subjective constitution.

DURING THE LAST LECTURE, we attempted to answer the question which, during a moving afternoon at the *praetorium*, the pure politician, the exemplification of pure frivolity, asked the Son of Man, the pure heart: *Quid est veritas?*

And yet this question, like so many others, is a multicolored affair, for we may seek thereby to determine the nature of truth, or its composition, or the set of factors on which it may depend. But then again, we may be simply trying to establish what we understand by truth. We may note that the two senses of the question are intrinsically very different, and also that the tasks involved in answering them promise to be of unparalleled difficulty. Indeed, we have addressed only the second sense, which in fact involves the easiest and most urgent issue: what is the meaning of truth? All other aspects of the question, which were left aside (e.g., the nature of truth, or its composition, or the set of factors on which it may depend, or the manner of gaining access to it), are at least subject to one indefeasible condition, namely, that the answers they may lead us to shall present us with the same thing that is disclosed by our understanding of truth, and not with something else.

[There is] an ambiguity about the expression "true for me." Truth [as] "quality" . . .

In my belief that A is B, I find the quality "truth." Just as I said before that A is B, I now say that belief α is true or exhibits truth. Someone could retort that the quality "truth" is also the content of a belief, the believing act involved being like the sense of assuredness which, in a way analogous to sadness or joy, adheres to [a content.]

The relativity of pleasure and displeasure (Plato).

Pain and pleasure cannot be put together in one whole.

The sense of evidence is something of this sort.

Not at all: there is a sense of hesitation in regard to unsuspected evidence.

[Consider the following example:] "Now I am seeing a blackboard." [Here we may distinguish between] my [act of] thinking, what I am thinking, and the things thought about. My thinking as opposed to my seeing: what I think is the ideal or conceptual form of what I see. My act of seeing or of visual perception delivers things to me. What I understand as a result of my having thought something is found by me in my visual experience: I note, then, that what I think and the things given to me in visual experience are identical. The evidential act is the means by which I see or find the identity in question. Just as in visual experience I see colors, in the evidential act I see the identity between what I think and the things [about which I think].

Every truth is grounded in an evidential act. [Someone could say that] things are not in themselves just the way they are given to me in perception. Fine, [I would reply,] and yet the things thought by my act of thinking are precisely those which my perception discloses, and not others to which I made no reference and about which I know absolutely nothing. . . .

Accordingly, there is no question here of a subjective impulse motivating me to declare that my thoughts about things are true; on the contrary, the things [themselves] are the warrants which justify my thoughts.

The truth that two and two makes four rests with the two itself and the repetition of it.

[A question of] relativism: would the inhabitant of the star Sirius perhaps think that two and two make five? [The matter of the subject's] "constitution."

Perhaps there is no science of mathematics on Sirius, but if there is, if the inhabitant of Sirius thinks of two (i.e., the two about which we humans think) and if he mentally performs the repetition of two, what sense would there be to saying that truth would be otherwise for him?

If, strictly speaking, something is true for me, then it will be absolutely true.

[What about] truth in the land of the blind? It is not that they see things in a way different from ours; it is only that they do not see them at all. Truths about colors do not exist for them.

[They have] different worlds and a different bodily constitution, but their worlds are not opposite to ours.

(Three-dimensional) bodies are given in perspective. Now then, if they exist for God, they will exist for God in that fashion [too].

A transformation of the subjectivistic stance: where my eye is, no other is found; what my eye sees, any other does not; therefore, my truth is not your truth.

[But] such [is] not at all [the case]. To be sure, where I am, nobody [else] is; the world doubtless delineates itself for me, and acquires a look which only I can perceive. And yet this does not signify that the world is otherwise than I say and see it to be. All aspects and perspectives really belong to the object.

Ideal objects (those for which time and space are immaterial) do not manifest themselves through a necessary multiplication in appearance in the same sense [as bodies]. The organ which perceives objects of this sort (the intellect) is characterized—in some sense—by its omnipresence and capacity for understanding. The earth as an ideal object vs. the earth as a visual object: it is the latter which offers itself by way of specific appearances available only to me. Herein lies a truth which is about things, precisely on the basis of my own uniqueness.

Organic constitution [as] an instrument of analysis. The senses *qua* sensuous dimensions of the world: the senses project themselves into one another. [The example of] François Hüber and his bees. The sieve or sifter; *ta erotiká* [the objects of desire].

Mental constitution: attention as the directing and selective [power] which regulates the senses. Frame of mind *(tesitura)*. Sharks. The sort of object, and the sort of truth about objects, which may reach each shark is a function of the structure [of the animal]. For this reason the actual situation is the opposite of that propounded by Darwin and Lamarck. The being in question creates its own surrounding world; it selects it and gives it shape. Every individual [is] necessary; [it is] the focal point.

The individual *qua* organ and extended arm of the universe. The ethnic group; the nation.

The Spanish dimension of the world.

The genuine components or portions of the world are constituted in the various ethnic groups, historical periods, and individuals. The universe as such does not exist in anyone in particular, since every individual is a "unique standpoint." History is an inter-individual affair, resulting from integration of the various portions of the world. God *qua* integration [of perspectives], as the correlate of the universe (or *omnitudo veritatum* [the totality of truths]), consists in excluding every possible exclusion. God as a demand deriving from logic. If [there is] no [such requirement], *there is no physics* [at all].

In sum: anyone who does not persist in contradicting himself will have to say that "what is true for me" is true in itself or absolutely, instead of asserting that the true is "what is true for me."

The nature of the species [is that of] an *event*. Truth *qua* event: if so, truth does not exist.

[Edmund] Husserl and [the question of] the "nonexistence of human constitution and existence."

[The question of] the nonexistence of the world and, within it, of the ego and of the species. [It is] just a matter of chance that there are species constituted in such a way that the "world exists" for them. But species are understood to be products of the world, and yet the world depends on them—that is to say, the world is and is not on the basis of such species.

Errors of such magnitude presuppose great frivolity. . . . They amount to a lack of self-understanding.

Like ideal vessels which reach us from Ceylon with an overflow cargo of spices, our words go forth, transporting our inner life from soul to soul. A soul [hard as] bronze. Achilles.

Signification and sign. Being and sign. Signal and foundation. The ideal nexus present to consciousness.

[Is] the word a sign of mental life? A gesture, an emotive expression, a fit of crying, pallor. The consciousness of their expressive power is lacking. Physiognomy.

14

The subjectivistic, relativistic stance belongs to the past. Truth and knowledge: the ambiguity of truth. The kernel of psychology. Kinds of truth. The "conditions" of subjectivity. The spotlight [of attention]. The ideal goal of psychology.

WE WERE URGENTLY IN NEED of a first encounter with the subjectivistic, relativistic interpretation of the meaning of truth. As I have often reiterated since the beginning of the course, this is the position constituting the ideological climate in which our minds have taken shape, and so much so that it has become a sort of spiritual instinct in us. Moreover, it is obvious that this interpretation has at least become entrenched in philosophy, if indeed it has not come to form part of the general sensibility of the European soul. And yet no other attitude would be more fruitless for the work of the intellect than that of insistence on our abiding by yesterday's thoughts, when a new mode of thinking is already with us.

In this first encounter with relativism, I have limited myself to pointing out the intrinsic ambiguity in any view which makes the quality "truth" contingent upon the subject and his constitution—in any formula containing the expression "true for . . . ," whether the referent be man, an inhabitant of Alpha Centauri, or God himself. I have not claimed, however, either to have given expression to that ambiguity to the satisfaction of all, or to have eradicated relativism by means of my formulations.

It was unconvincing to argue that such a consequential quid pro quo could arise only and exclusively on the basis of the word "truth." Let us think of this term as one to which many other expressions contribute their own significations, expressions alike in that the delimitation of their meaning is most perilous. Truth was but a quality of cognition, and cognition presupposes a great many other concepts, such as those of thinking, reality, subject, consciousness, representation, mental content, etc. Having sprouted almost imperceptibly from one of these words, having blossomed in another, having become crowned with success in yet a third, having produced offspring in still a fourth, and so on, the ambiguity of which I speak explodes, finally and suddenly, in the minute body of the term "truth," which [at first glance] appears to be so harmless.

Only when we manage, step by step, to identify the origins of this ambiguity in every one of those elementary concepts can we claim to have completely fulfilled our goal, to have understood in full the meaning of such ambiguity. But, inasmuch as those concepts are fundamental to psychology, we would then have come unexpectedly to possess the key to this scientific discipline. All of a sudden, we would find ourselves having reached the very kernel of the science of psychology, while all along we thought to have spoken only of logic, metaphysics, and grammar.

In the lecture before last, I attempted to show that any theory wherein the quality "truth" is reduced to relativity is an absurdity, in the same sense as saying that I see green when I see blue is a contradiction. And I tried to accomplish that by analyzing the meaning of the expression "true for me." A contradiction is implicit in every position which denies that the true is absolutely true (on the assumption, of course, that there is truth) and which opposes the view

that what is true for me is true for any other subject, whatever his constitution (provided that the truth in question
indeed be the case and not one of my errors).

Now, the relativistic trend not only implies such a doc-
trinal absurdity; it also involves a well-founded purpose,
that of making us see that the human possession of the truth
is subject to obvious limitations. As a matter of fact, we
neither possess all truths nor can ever succeed in doing so.
In this sense, truth can indeed be called relative, and yet
this is a poor way to express the matter, for only the kinds
and the number of [achievable] truths are relative to man,
and not truth itself.

Accordingly, I was somewhat pressed to acknowledge
that this (certainly trivial) aspect of the relativistic position
is correct. To this purpose I devoted my last lecture. I now
wish to underscore the fact that what I did then was to
present—by way of the most far-reaching anticipation possible—a positive account of the influence exerted by the
subject on the truth. And I achieved this by adopting a
standpoint entirely free of relativism. But the results obtained then were only the sketch and outline of a theory,
not meant to be taken as a fully warranted and grounded
exposition.

But, I argued, how could it be denied that—in some sense
or other—the subject imposes conditions on truth? First of
all, the body plays a role in this by means of its sense organs:
the nervous system lies as an intermediary between our
consciousness and the universe, like a fine grid or sieve
which allows only a fragment of reality to come through,
while excluding the rest. Undoubtedly, the six-thousand-
facet eye of the golden bee and man's light-condensing eyeball grasp two different worlds. But is there any sense in
asking which of the two visual organs actually sees the visible
world as it truly is? The visible world exists in as many
ways as there are ways of seeing it: each one of those situated

around an object sees a different aspect and side of it, but the fact that such [appearances] are different from one another [does not mean] that they do not belong to the same object.

Accordingly, whatever worldly content reaches the subject does so, to begin with, as a function of the latter's organic structure, considered both specifically and individually. And yet the mental structure of the subject plays an even more decisive role in this affair.

[Consider the following.] For a man concerned with the sphere of mathematics, biological truths do not exist. A man of that sort is blind to religious or artistic problems, but is endowed with great perspicacity in discerning physical or chemical problems. Obviously, if something exists for us, if we notice it while we are oblivious to something else, the reason is—to put it in the usual way—that we are paying attention to it. But if the word "attention" is not to be used vaguely, and if we are eventually to come to terms with it, we shall have to regard it as nothing but the product of our own individual make-up.

We are all grouped together under the name "man," precisely because we coincide, for the most part, in our predispositions or—as I prefer to say—in our frame of mind *(tesitura)*. Part of my word is a possession common to all. I am referring to that portion of the whole with which the basic activities of life are concerned. Indeed, when someone does not coincide with us in those respects, we exclude him from out midst and consider him abnormal. Moreover, within the human species, each ethnic group constitutes itself as a particular compact company of men by virtue of shared ways and their characteristic manners of being normal. Finally, we come to the individual man who alone can intuit and see certain truths and realities. He may eventually succeed in communicating part of this unique endowment to others, by rendering it accessible to them in some form of quasi-intuitive experience, i.e., by indirect means such as words. And yet there will always be a residue which remains unexpressed and is practically inexpressible and therefore incommunicable. This is the psychological root for the phenomenon of radical solitude into which human beings grow as they become increasingly more individualized. Thus we come to discover the inevitable dimension of unintelligibility and incommunicability which constitutes the last horizon of the deepest friendships and the most faithful love relationships. Every individual is a perceptual organ which can apprehend something that escapes the rest of mankind, and is like an extended arm which alone reaches into certain depths of the universe that remain unknown to others. No image is more fitting to express the relationship between our consciousness and the world of realities and truths than this: in the midst of the night at sea, a vessel's spotlight wanders about the dark and fixes itself suddenly on this or that bit of cloud in the skies.

By way of outline, here you have what, in my opinion, is the problem with which the science of psychology is concerned. While other disciplines are engaged in the orderly gathering of truths about the world which each man has been able so far to tear away from the universe, psychology turns its back on such truths and on the world, and devotes itself to the study of the mechanism and structure of each subjective consciousness. We may examine either the colors of the landscape or the eye that sees them. Turning away from the world, psychology studies the psyche, the organ with which we perceive the world.

But the ideal goal pursued by psychology would ultimately be the determination of the unique or idiosyncratic dimensions of the mental make-up of a Newton, i.e., of the subjective constitution which permitted the notion of the science of mechanics to get caught and trapped in his mind, or of the soul of a Cervantes. . . .

All I have done here is to present a few examples, behind which lie concealed extended series of problems. Psychology had run aground in analyzing some of them, without being able either to advance or to justify a retreat. We could have detected in the laboratories devoted to psychological research and in the reflections of psychologists a kind of despair and sloth *(acedia)*, a sort of *odium professionis* [hatred for the calling, or profession], similar to that which usually overcomes a monk when the first fires of his religious ardor have become extinguished.

But in the last few years springtime has unexpectedly arrived in the field of psychology. Beyond the shadow of a doubt, this transformation has been brought about by the publication of Edmund Husserl's *Logical Investigations* in 1900[–1901].

And the most fruitful of all the good choices made in that work was the reinstitution—nay, the initiation, in a certain sense—of the inquiries concerning the nature of meaning.

15

Language. "Meaning." Sensation and perception. The law of sense-perceptual contamination. Assimilation. Perception and sensation. Description.

THE STUDY OF LANGUAGE—an enterprise promising to bring about, in my estimation, the most profound modifications to psychological theory—encompasses an unpredictable number of component problems. Among them, we find the methodological question of establishing the boundary lines between the science of language and what I would call, broadly speaking, the philosophy of language. What are the respective jurisdictional spheres of linguist and philosopher concerning the phenomena of language? Even within the philosophy of language, we shall have to settle a number of jurisdictional disputes. If, as I believe, it is possible to cultivate a science dealing with the pure forms of meaning (one which would study, for instance, the roles of noun and adjective and the a priori laws at the basis of such functions), if, in other words, a general and a priori grammar is possible in principle, then we shall have to inquire into the possibility of clearly distinguishing its subject matter from that of an empirical psychology bent on examining the individual and collective mental facts in which language becomes embodied. In the context, then, of the philosophy of language, we shall have to distinguish between general grammar and the psychology of language. But even if we do this, we shall have left out of consideration the main problem, the question concerning the nature of language *in genere*. Both psychologist and grammarian must presuppose the fundamental concept of the word, or the nature of the linguistic function, if they are indeed to examine the concrete facts and pure forms in which such a notion finds its verification. Accordingly, there will have to be an essential science of language or a discipline concerned with the essence of language, namely, a noology of meaning, or what I have called semiology.

Let this quick overview of the differences between such disciplines serve to indicate the multifarious problems which are provoked in philosophy simply by exploration of the phenomenon of speech. In any case, linguists already have plenty to examine when they notice that in just a minute or so, a man can clearly utter approximately two thousand sounds, that there are at least a thousand languages, and that the grammar of only one of them (in a sense, the most complete grammar available, that composed for Sanskrit by the Indian Panini in the third [*sic*] century B.C.[1]) contains four thousand rules.

At this point, we need to have a first clear glimpse of what a word is, so as not to come to terms with it [merely] as something we hear or see. There is a coleopterous insect, known as the *Bostrychos typographus*, which leaves behind a trail most closely resembling writing, and yet we do not take such traces to be writing. By contrast, [when we see] a printed text, the visual sensations of the marks are accompanied by something which is neither line nor color. In the purely visual object referred to as a "letter," we already find—as a sort of precipitate or sediment—a mental or intentional act, characterizable as an "act of meaning." What do I see when I look at the sign "earth" on the blackboard? Let me answer this question in paradoxical terms, for what is involved is a paradox indeed. What I see is not what, strictly speaking, I am seeing, namely, the wavy chalk line standing out against the black surface, but rather a "meaning," which is even more conspicuous than the chalk marks and which, so to speak, rests and rides on them.

In employing the word "meaning," we have made use of an expedient to get out of a difficulty. Do you appreciate the problem? Suppose we had not been satisfied with that vague term and had attempted to describe more accurately and concretely the shadowy object we found implanted in the white chalk line. . . . But what is it? I do not claim to be able to answer this question completely, and any chance of success is even smaller because I can devote only a few words to it in the time allotted to us. For the time being, we shall have to be content with the strong impression which the shadowy object may make on us, since clear knowledge of it is out of our reach [in this context]. For this purpose, let us look again at the shapes traced along its trail by *Bostrychos typographus*. What we do not see in those configurations, but do see and find in the sign "earth," is precisely that which transforms a mere visual image into a word. We term such [a difference] "meaning," and yet the fact that we assign a name to it does not signify that we know what it is. *Qu[a]eritur equidem!* [This is indeed the question!][2]

Some among you, on the basis of the traditional ideas you possess in the field of psychology, may perhaps think that "meaning"—whatever it may be—would obviously consist of some mental or perhaps ideal stuff, but not of anything which could possibly be regarded as color. Now then, we see colors and only colors. How is it, then, that anyone could say—except by way of inappropriate metaphor—that we see "meaning" in conjunction with the white tracing of the letters?

This point is well taken. In fact, the traditional psychologist would ask this question. But with all due respect, I must charge him with making up things instead of engaging in inquiry, for he does not make an effort to regard matters just and precisely as they are and present themselves to be, a procedure which, if followed, sometimes proves to be quite unsettling for our preconceived ideas. Rather, the traditional psychologist prescribes, before the fact, how matters *should* and *must* be, and only on the basis of this prescription does he approach the objects in question, consequently remaining blind to whatever belies his own preconception. For many years, I devoted my life to the practice of a particular philosophy, an experience which, in my opinion, has been most fortunate for my philosophical education. I am referring to Neo-Kantianism, a school of thought which, self-avowedly and resolutely, regarded things not as they *are*, but as they *should* be. I am, then, too well acquainted with that stance to take it for granted now, when it is not a question of finding out what philosophers have said, but of inquiring into what things are.

In addressing myself to such a remark, therefore, I would have to say so many things that even two weeks would not be sufficient to bring our venture to a conclusion. I in fact believe that, without any metaphorical admixture, I *do see* the meaning "earth" in the wavy line itself which belongs to the sign "earth." Now, to render my assertion completely plausible, I would have to develop in its entirety the theoretical account of perception. Such a development indeed constitutes one of the most suggestive, attractive, and even dramatic undertakings possible, but this is not the place for it.

On this occasion, I will limit myself to making the following point. "Seeing" may be regarded in two different ways. Either we understand by the term the experience by which we have light or chromatic sensations, or we take it to signify what it commonly means to us, namely, the act of consciousness by which we encounter the things of the material surrounding world (e.g., the table, the house, the man, or the moon). Before deciding which of the two senses of the word to accept, you will find it useful to anticipate the consequences of your choice. Understood as the act by which we merely possess chromatic sensations, seeing would not involve our visually grasping anything at all. Who among you has ever seen pure chromatic sensations [*sensa*]? You have always seen a color in something, i.e., adhering to the thing, materialized and fulfilled on it. Furthermore, we see a color occupying some determinate place and located some distance away from our retina. Moreover, we see it extending on a surface. Now then, neither the matter to which the color is inseparably joined, nor the distance separating it from us, nor its property of extending [on a surface] is itself color. Neither things nor their shapes nor the distances pertaining to objects are colors. Accordingly, we are forced to conclude that we do not see things [at all], or [even] their shapes or distances. But this is precisely the meaning of the [apparently] prudent remark to which I referred above, and which I took to be implicitly addressed to me [by some of you]. This view, I believe, must now appear to you as even more strange than my contention that we *do see* "meaning" in the white tracing itself.

In technical terms, we would have to say that the two senses or values of "seeing" are seeing *qua* sensation and seeing *qua* perception. I perceive things, and in them, as their countenance and features, I perceive their colors, which I call objective colors, since they belong in the objects and are found in them. But I only feel heat. I do not perceive it as such, that is to say, I do not see it. I see things by means of my chromatic sensations, on the basis of which my consciousness proceeds, although such sensations are neither the counterpart nor the object of consciousness. Colors present things to me. Indeed, the purpose of every sensation is to present to us in terms of distance and shape that which cannot be sensed as *res* [thing].

But as I said before, were we to engage in the examination of these matters, there would be no end to it. [Instead, let us do something else.] To get some idea of the nature of pure color, just think of the difference between what the painter is trying to see and in fact translates on canvas, and what we normally see on the canvas. The painter has not seen as we do the apple that appears to us in Eve's hand. On the contrary, he has undone, so to speak, the appearance which the apple naturally displays before our sight. He has averted his glance from the real thing "apple", and instead set himself after the minimal aspects and nuances of color, which are precisely what we [usually] give no mind to. If the apple appears yellow to us, it is nevertheless many-colored to him. He does us the service, then, of displaying on canvas the chromatic materials in which, through which, or by means of which, we in fact see the apple.

In [examining] the reflections [of light], you may find still another clue to assist you in understanding the difference between pure and objective color. [Consider] the reflections which, as mystical spears of light, are cast by a well-polished object, especially one made of metal or glass. We do not take them as colors belonging to the object; they never assimilate themselves to the thing, or become part of it. We see them over the thing, so to speak, as emerging or radiating from it—or, to be more exact, as existing in the area between the thing and us. Reflections are almost pure colors, and precisely for this reason we do not see them very well; in fact, as is well known, they "dazzle" or "blind" us. Often this happens not because there is too much light, [but rather because of something like this:] since we fail to locate the reflections swiftly and skillfully, the eyeball hesitates, and it tries out—in quick succession—several positions (although without finding any one of them satisfactory), inasmuch as localization depends on the self-adjustment of the eyeball. Herein originates the tremor in the eye when we are dazzled, as well as the resulting act by which we avert our glance and redirect it toward a steadier and more definite thing, concerning which the eyeball can produce a relatively stable adjustment. (The golden aura. The irreality of reflections. [The experience of] foreshortening. The [optical] illusion of the dihedral angle).

We may notice, then, the way in which sense-percepti-bility—the property of serving as visual evidence—carries over to elements which are not themselves colors, although it originates with purely chromatic sensation. And if this occurs in the case of color, the equivalent happens with sound (e.g., the sound of a streetcar).

In my view, such phenomena, to which so little attention was devoted until recently, are decisive for the rectification [needed] in psychology and, in a certain sense, in physiology as well, although this is not the place to indicate the reasons. I have come to believe that we must establish a basic law concerning one of the fundamental questions about the psyche. I would call it the law of sense-perceptual contamination, and it would read as follows: in every act of consciousness in which nonsensuous components are given together with a sensuous element, a primordial tendency exists by which the characteristic property of the latter, sense-perceptibility, carries over and is transferred to the former. In this fashion, for example, that which is strictly visual in the object endows the totality with visibility.

To be sure, such a law does not explain anything, but then again it does not imply that it will do so. It merely describes a phenomenon of general import precisely as a phenomenon. It therefore belongs within the scope of de-scriptive psychology, like anything else that is contained in this course or in the one which is to follow it.[3] An explan-atory psychology will not be able to proceed successfully unless the phenomena it seeks to explain are well defined. I shall use the name "description" to refer to that process by which we seek to establish the boundaries of an imme-diate appearance or of a phenomenon *qua* phenomenon. If one compares a treatise of physics with those devoted to experimental psychology, one will notice that the assertions in the latter are characterized by a pervasive vagueness, even though the same methods of investigation are employed in both. In my opinion, the vagueness of the explanatory laws arises from the vagueness [with which] problems are posed in the science of psychology. We shall not be able to avoid confusion in the formulation of these problems until we take to heart the task of methodically describing phenomena. Since the Renaissance, science has been concerned more with explaining than with describing. Such an undertaking has been fruitful in those fields of research where human spontaneous and living observation had accumulated beforehand a great many clear distinctions pertaining to physical Nature. But no [comparable][4] attainment is identifiable in the progress made since the Renaissance in the sciences of biology, psychology, sociology, history, ethics, or aesthetics, disciplines in which—for obvious reasons—spontaneous reflection has not been as abundant as in the physical sciences. During the nineteenth century, the desire for explanatory accounts reached a state of frenzy in some fields—evolutionary biology, for instance. An interest in description, however, was being born in other areas. Among the latter, mathematics, which is nothing but a descriptive science. The success obtained has been so great that mathematical knowledge, [according to Henri] Bergson, has multiplied a hundredfold.

But let us return to the subject of our concern. We were speaking of the law of sense-perceptual contamination. According to it, whenever sensuous elements play an essential role in an act, their sensuous character is transmitted to the nonsensuous components and, therefore, to the whole. As opposed to the doctrine of associationism, the [employment of the] explanatory concept of assimilation, which plays such an important role in [Wilhelm] Wundt's psychological accounts, is tantamount to having taken one step in the direction of [formulating] the law in question.

To my mind, however, the most interesting aspect of this law is the fact that it makes apparent the proper role of sensation. Since [John] Locke, but especially since [George] Berkeley and [David] Hume, sensations have been [regarded]—in the science of psychology—as the primary content of consciousness. In other words, [according to this position], we are always conscious of a group of sensations, or have them as the correlate or terminus of our consciousness. Hence, inasmuch as sensations are subjective states, the primary and immediate content of consciousness is subjective. And since the only thing I directly find and advert to is my own ego, the objective world is attained only through my subjectivity, i.e., mediately and secondarily, or merely fictively. Adherence to this thesis is the original sin committed by modern subjectivism, a stance to which I have referred so often.

But the thesis is completely erroneous, the exact opposite of the truth.

When I see an apple or a house, I see anything but my subjective states. I do not see my own chromatic sensations, but [only] colors [extending] in space and embodied and materialized in [the apple or] the house. Or to put it in general terms: the primordial content of any act of consciousness is always constituted by the correlate or terminus of the act in question (by what I see, or hear, or think), but the act itself is never given to me in any way or fashion. In order to encounter it, I must reflectively disassemble the object seen: in my thoughts I must analyze it and resolve it into its components. As the last residue of such a resolution, I would then encounter the sensations with which, or in which, I previously saw the object, my sensations being therefore the result of a process of abstraction.

Let me now summarize what I have said, but not without

first urging you to give some thought to the formulae I employ. What we perceive (i.e., the real thing, as endowed with shape, as separated by a distance [from other things and from us], and so on) is not sensory in nature. What is sensory in nature (i.e., the sensations themselves) is not perceptible at all. It follows, therefore, that the sensations do not play the role of components or parts of objects. The sensations merely present or actualize the latter in our consciousness; they just symbolize objects. (Locations in space and our muscular feeling of adjustment [to them] are somehow incongruous, [as in] a story by Poe.) Sensation, then, is endowed with a symbolic function. But what is the point of all this?

Our purpose was to understand the nature of the word, i.e., its verbal or expressive function. I remarked that a word is not a word by virtue of its sound or [visual] configuration. Rather, its value as a word is a function of something else, which is attached to the sound and configuration. We have always believed that the role of sign is the aspect of the word which exists above and beyond its sound dimension. We may still find this belief [embodied in the work of] J. Stuart Mill, and also in that of [Christoph] Sigwart, [Theodor] Ziehen, Jodl,[5] and Wundt. In sum, we see it prevail in almost the entire history of psychology (whether ancient, medieval, or contemporary).

Over against this traditional opinion, I introduced you to another more perceptive approach, in which the problem is raised as to whether the indicative and expressive functions of the word are one and the same. The most distinguished representative of this position is [Edmund] Husserl, although he is by no means the first proponent of it. Even though Husserl is not very fond of citing his living forerunners, I must point out that the main distinctions on which his work is based are found in an article published by [Anton] Marty in 1884.

I have already outlined the manner of approach chosen by Husserl to deal with this matter.[6] We begin by recognizing certain phenomena, such as those of smoke[7] and gesticulation, the perception of which leads us to some belief, in this instance that there is fire and a given emotional state. If we put together this fact with the role which premisses play in our minds with regard to conclusions, namely, that believing in the former is a ground for believing in the latter as well, it follows that in our awareness of signs, the object performing the role of pointing to and the object denoted or pointed at are given to us by two different acts of consciousness, one of which is the motive or ground for the other. Moreover, for something to play the role of sign, the object pointed to must not be an immediate object of consciousness: we should gain access to it precisely *by means of* the object performing the role of sign.

Now then, Husserl contends that when I hear or read a word, the object immediately grasped by my consciousness is the word itself, by which I then come to notice or assume the existence of a mental state in the subject who speaks or writes to me (such noticing or assuming being a mediate form of awareness). But, Husserl continues, a word is not merely a man's way of addressing another, since it also has a role to perform in single, solitary mental life. Not only do I address my words to another man; I also engage in speech when I think to myself. In a very suggestive book, a Frenchman named St. Paul has referred to this use of speech as the *endophasic* employment of language.[8] But it makes no sense to speak of a word used in endophasis as a sign. First of all, what I am here talking about is my own intellectual performance (for example, my act of forming a concept, my judging, or my reasoning), and that performance is given to me as immediately as is the inner image of the word. I am in no need to discover the fact that I am thinking. Second, a word performing its genuine function in the single, solitary life of consciousness does not become the correlate or terminus of the individual's mental act. When the word "Napoleon," say, arises in my mind, I think not of it, but of the historical personage who went by that name. My consciousness is busy with the man Napoleon; my mind is thus concerned with him and not with the verbal image of the man. We clearly see this difference when we cease considering the term "Napoleon" in its signifying function and begin to examine it under the aspect of what the Scholastics used to call *suppositio materialis* [material supposition]. In a study of that sort, we deal with the word "Napoleon" in the fashion of grammarians. We are left with the corpse of a verbal image; the pure signifying power has escaped from it, and we are confronted only with what remains—a word no longer, but a mere phonetic occurrence.

As Husserl then concluded, and Marty had done before him, the word, as used in conversation or dialogue, is in fact a sign of the mental act performed by the speaker. In the word, understood in this manner, the other's thought achieves external expression. We realize this fact in a way similar to that of harboring the suspicion that whenever we see smoke, there is fire. Such is what I would call the communicative function of language, and nothing more. If expression means for us only externalization, that is to say, the event of instituting a sign or signal, then the communicative function of language would be its expressive [function].

> The many bodily sensations,
> the human heart's own feelings,
> and even our ideal aspirations,
> by the organs of the voice
> gain "expression" in parlances diverse.

These, ladies and gentlemen, are verses, or, at least, things of this sort were so regarded around the year 1780, when Tomás [de] Iriarte composed his splendid "Poem on Music," the beginning of the first part of which I have just quoted. And in such verses the word "expression" signifies the manner in which we convey our thoughts to each other by means of the organs of the voice.[9]

Appendices

	Real [or Simple] Objects (e.g., a "rose")	Imaginary Objects (e.g., a centaur)	Ideal Objects (e.g., a triangle)	Impossible Objects (e.g., a square circle)	[The question is:] Whether or not they are (ontology)
Structural Objects (e.g., a rose's being-white)		The opponent [is]	A rose's not-being-white		
Noetic Acts ([e.g., that corresponding to] "the rose is white")		The opposite [is]	"The rose is not white"		Whether or not they are true (logic)
Sentences (e.g., "The rose is white")		The contradictory [is]	"The rose is not white"		Whether or not they are meaningful (semiology)
Values	They exhibit positive or negative worth				(axiology)

Noology

Table, as referred to on pp. 248 and 249.

Toward a Philosophical Dictionary

1: Abstraction

If we take this word as a philosophical term, we have to distinguish between two senses. First, we have "abstraction" understood as a logical operation or method; second, we take it as the name for a psychological mechanism.

In logic, abstraction is the process by which we suppress one or more elements in the meaning of a concept, the result being a different concept with a smaller intension and a greater extension [than the original]. If, conducting ourselves in this manner, we disregard certain physical and moral characteristics found in the concept "Spaniard," we are left with the concept "European," which contains fewer determinations than "Spaniard" and, reciprocally, refers to a much larger group of men. By the process of abstraction, we constitute the species on the basis of the concept of the individual, and we form the genus on the basis of the species. If we proceed in the opposite direction, we increase the number of elements in the concept and go down from genus to individual. This is the logical method, opposite to abstraction, which is called determination.

Logical abstraction, then, constitutes (*es*) an ideal conceptual order, which is established as a function of the greater or lesser content, or of the greater or lesser number of elements [in the make-up of the concepts which form part of the order in question]. Of course, terms like "greater," "lesser," and "number" of elements, and, in general, terms which directly express mathematical values, may be applied only indirectly or metaphorically to the relations between concepts found in the order of abstraction and determination. Instead, we could use terms like "implication" or "non-implication" [to give expression] to the conceptual relations [here under consideration. Accordingly, we could say that] the species implies the genus, that is to say, that the elements making up the genus are part of the complete set constituting the species. The elements which are components of the generic concept do not, on the contrary, imply those which are constituents of the specific concepts. And yet it is an essential function of the genus to "ex-plicate" itself, i.e., to unfold into various species. Therefore, using "implication," in a sense which is qualitatively other than the one just employed a moment ago, we can say that the genus implies the species, that it contains them, [so to speak,] as if preformed within itself.

This second kind of implication gives rise to the serious problems that beset the method of abstraction. "Color," [for example,] is a genus; "red," "blue," and "yellow" are species of this genus. Each color species in turn diversifies itself into "shades" or "hues," [thus constituting] the last level of differentiation of which the genus is capable. The content of a given visual perception is the intuitive reality of a completely individual "color." In other words, the *real* color is *one* of the shades of *one* of the species of color. Only in "shade" or "hue" do we then find a concept adequate to intuitive reality. We see the [given] shade, but [we do not see] "red," which already is an *abstract* variation (*tonalidad*), a *class* of hues. It would then be even less reasonable to say that we see "color." Seen or real color, as we clearly encounter it upon opening our eyes or in the exercise of our phantasy, is an individual object. When we say "red," we are referring, on the contrary, to an object altogether different from what *each* individual red could possibly be. We are not now referring to *this* or *that* red, and we are not even talking about *all* the reds. Or to express it with greater clarity: if in actual perception we were at any point to be conscious of all the reds, we would then be aware of a set of individual objects. Now then, we could increase or decrease the membership of such a set, but we could never, by this means, come to be confronted with the object "red." Over against the multiplicity of *all* reds, this object is one. [*Mutatis mutandis*,] the same situation would hold for the object "color."

Hence, species and genera are not given to us either in perception or in intuitive representation [i.e., in phantasy]. And yet we cannot assert that the specific and generic objects are mere sums or collections of individual objects. We must see this to come to terms with the perennial questions concerning the relations between the *general*, on the one hand, and the individual and the collective, on the other.

Let us keep alive to the obvious differences—irremovable by any conceivable argument—which exist between the objects referred to by the following expressions: "an *A*," "several *A*'s," "all *A*'s," and "*A*."

Now then, the question of whether or not there are general objects has been subject to the strangest vicissitudes in the history of philosophy. (In the present context, I employ the term "object" to denote anything endowed with a determination of its own.)

The controversy concerning this matter reappears in the Modern Era in connection with [John] Locke's doctrine of abstract ideas. To put it in [Edmund] Husserl's words:

> [According to the English philosopher, in] actual reality nothing like a universal exists; only individual things, arranged into genera and species, by their exact or less exact resemblances, have real existence. If we remain within the sphere of what is immediately given and experienced, in the sphere of "ideas" in Locke's sense, phe-

nomenal things are complexes of "simple ideas," in which the same simple ideas, the same phenomenal attributes, recur simply or in groups. Things now receive names, and not merely proper names, but for the most part common names; the fact that many things can be un-ambiguously named by one and the same universal name, shows that a universal sense or "idea" must correspond to such a name.

If we consider how the general name applies to the objects of the pertinent class, it becomes plain that it does so because one and the same attribute (or complex of attri-butes) is common to all these objects. The univocality of the universal name extends only as far as objects are named by way of this and no other attribute (or *idea* of an attribute).

The universal thought carried out in such universal mean-ings therefore presupposes that we have the *power of ab-straction*, i.e., the power to separate off partial ideas, ideas of such attributes, from the phenomenal things given to us as complexes of attributes, and to associate them with words of which they are the general meanings.[1]

Consequently, the abstract idea would contain something which is not found by itself in reality, since it is a product, "artifact," or "invention" of ours. And yet the task of form-ing such general ideas is not so free of difficulty as it may seem at first glance. As Locke says:

. . . does it not require some pains and skill to form the *general idea* of a *triangle* (which is yet none of the most abstract, comprehensive, and difficult), for it must be neither oblique nor rectangle, neither equilateral, equi-crural, nor scalenon; but all and none of these at once [?]. In effect, it is something imperfect that cannot exist, an *idea* wherein some parts of several different and inconsistent *ideas* are put together. It is true, the mind in this imperfect state has need of such *ideas*, and makes all the haste to them it can, for the conveniency of communication and enlargement of knowledge.[2]

Herein lies so strange a mixture of truth and error that it is understandable that Locke's doctrine has been—to this day—a bone of contention in English philosophy. First of all, in referring to ideas which are—or which at least claim to be—"general," it is not convenient to employ the name "abstract idea" simply on the grounds that their origin is due to our power of abstraction. More serious, however, is the ambiguity in the way [Locke] uses the term "idea," which did eventually become part and parcel of the tradition of British thought. When Locke speaks of the idea of a right-angled triangle, he is referring to the real image which we have, or may have, [in our minds]. But upon using the same formula in dealing with *a* triangle *in general*, he does not notice the resulting contradiction, namely, that of asserting that we would have a real image of a triangle which is no particular triangle at all. If by "general idea" we were only to understand a real image of the sort called "triangle," no further pronouncement as to the nonexistence of general ideas would be needed. Since the term would then refer only to a sense-perceptible or imaginable singular, an idea could of course never be general. Locke's assertions, literally understood, do contain such an absurd notion, and it is precisely the literal sense of his words which has been the butt of subsequent empiricists, with Bishop Berkeley at the head of the pack. And yet one can easily discover the intent underlying the literal sense of the words. However circumspectly, Locke wishes to point to the possibility of another meaning for the term "idea," such that both general and individual notions could be regarded as ideas, although in

different senses. An individual idea is a sensuous representation, a real content of consciousness, an intuition of what
is present in the mind. We would be unable to *think* of or
to refer mentally to the triangle in general, unless in phantasy we could represent a particular triangle to ourselves.
And yet, as a matter of fact, whenever we *have* before our
minds a given particular triangle, we are not thinking of it
at all; rather we refer thereby to the genus "triangle." Such
an imaginary triangle is just *one* case of the genus in question,
and it can never become identical with it.

Husserl—from whom we have taken this presentation and
critique of Locke's position—has proposed a most consequential distinction, one which, despite its apparent insig-
nificance, is destined to transform the way in which most
psychological and epistemological problems are dealt with.
Thinking, contends Husserl, is an intentive or intentional
act, an act by which we refer to an object. "Meaning" is
precisely this reference. [Consider the following example.]
"Tree" is a meaning by which we refer to the object so
called. Now then, the meaning "tree" is different from
meanings such as "this tree" or "the Christmas tree." These
various significations tend toward, or refer to, different objects. That the object we refer to by "this tree" *could also be*
[meant as] "a tree in general" is now no source of major
difficulty. Likewise, when we say "tree," we are obviously
referring not to the object [denoted by] "this tree," i.e., the
one located here, in front of me, but to an object which is,
in itself, general, namely, the nature *tree* or *treeness*. This
realization does not result from any argument, nor could all
the arguments conceivable ever remove the immediately
available evidence that *what* I am thinking about or *understanding* as "tree" is quite different from *what* I am thinking
about as "this tree," "the other tree," or "a tree."

Now then, the meaning "tree," or that sense by which I
intentively refer to this particular object, needs some sup-

port or other from a real content of consciousness in order to *be realized*. [For instance,] the image of a poplar would *fulfill*, satisfy, or verify the meaning intention "tree." Note that no adequate correspondence exists between the object intended or understood ("tree") and the object really imagined (the poplar). The intuitive image only partially fulfills the intentive act, and yet it sufficiently verifies the thinking of "tree." By contrast, the meaning "the tree I saw yesterday" is fulfilled exactly and totally whenever the intuitive representation of the remembered object awakens in me. In this case, meaning and intuition coincide with and cover one another.

Now we can clearly see the confusion that Locke is responsible for. He wanted to find the genus "triangle" in consciousness, as a content which would be real in the same sense as a particular triangle is. It so happens that being given intuitively is only the way individual objects have of presenting themselves in consciousness, but it *is not the only way* available to consciousness in its business of referring to objects. The capital error of contemporary psychology consists in not being aware of this distinction.

Not recognizing the difference in question, thinkers have wasted many an effort in the attempt, after Locke, to reduce [the mental dimension of] ideality to the status of the intuitive. [They have tried to do so] by subjecting Locke's position in this regard to a critique, and yet at the same time they have preserved his tendency to ground what we call general ideas in the mental performance of abstraction. The generic triangle is an abstract object,[3] that is to say, it is a general object, the [dimension of] generality being [just] a component of the individual and inseparable therefrom. For this reason we cannot have it represented separately; we really come to have it only in its various individualizations. Accordingly, if we are incapable of having the general represented by itself or on its own, such a situation is not due, as Locke thought, to our own imperfection but is rooted in the essence of the general. Let it not be said, in a skeptical vein, that we should harbor doubts concerning the certainty [of our knowledge of] that essence. The essence of the general unfortunately implies that the general cannot be presented by itself. Such, [in any case,] is a condition to be met as well by [other] objects, the existence of which cannot be doubted. Take, for instance, a sound: its intensity cannot be heard apart from its quality. [Or consider the case of] color: it cannot be seen apart from the surface upon which it extends, and vice versa.

The absurdity in Locke's position when he spoke of a triangle in general as present really and intuitively *in* our consciousness led Berkeley even to deny the existence of general ideas, or of what we call general meanings. Nevertheless, he proceeded to explain the undeniable aspiration of our consciousness to understand certain objects as general, and [he tried to do so] by appealing to the psychological mechanism of abstraction.

Since then, we have not abandoned this way of thinking. German idealism placed itself, as a matter of course, within the realm of general meanings or ideas, without feeling itself to be urgently called to answer the question of whether they exist for human consciousness. By virtue of such inspired naïveté, it was able—with Kant—to make progress in the realm of ontological thought. However, the concern with psychological explication or clarification persisted in England, where it was the almost exclusive interest of philosophy. There, the real or presumed role of producing the general was assigned to the mental mechanism of abstraction.

Abstraction is the outcome of the mental act of paying attention. Attention is a specific event which consists in focusing the mental activity of seeing on a determinate sector, singled out from the totality of content confronting sight. Within the field of every actual consciousness, there is a center or axis of perceptual awareness and a peripheral zone. The existence of this phenomenal distinction is evident, whatever the explanation proposed for it may be. The particular content which is so selected (the content which coincides with the perceptual center or axis) is endowed with greater clarity and a sort of emphasis. [As a result,] this content stands out over against the rest of what is present; the emphasis placed on it is rendered manifest *in the content* itself, because it becomes relatively separate from whatever is surrounding it.

Availing himself of this recourse, [John] Stuart Mill denied the existence of general objects. [For him] there are no things in the objective world which are general in nature; and neither is there anything in consciousness which is really general, as Locke used to believe. The so-called general ideas do not exist; we are unable to represent to ourselves attributes, such as whiteness or humanity, if we mean to take them separately or by themselves. We find them

> solely as forming, in combination with numerous other attributes, the idea of an individual object. But, though thinking them only as part of a larger agglomeration, we *have the power of fixing our attention on them*, to the neglect of the other attributes with which we think them combined. While the concentration of attention actually lasts, if it is sufficiently intense, we may be temporarily unconscious of any of the other attributes, and may really, for a brief interval, have nothing present to our mind but the attributes constituent of the concept.[4]

According to this theory, then, no "general" attribute can ever be represented by itself, and yet we can pay attention to it. We are able, [for example,] to focus our attention on one or several of the attributes of a specific triangle present in our imagination. Or we can concern ourselves with the color of an orange. And such a possibility is open to us in the case of any triangle or any orange we may think of. By associating a name with an attribute, we are able—whenever we hear the name—to focus our attention on the attribute, and place emphasis thereon, within the totality of content present to us at the given juncture.

It is obvious that in this theory the real problem [to be considered] disappears by sleight of hand. An attempt is made to substitute a psychological mechanism for the special feature "generality," by dissolving in the former whatever may be characteristic about the latter. But I wonder whether the factor of attention is, in essence, sufficient to take upon itself the task of generalization. In representation, the only sort of thing given to me is the individual object. If I pay attention to only a part of it, if I place the axis of my perceptual awareness through a component or element of it, the part in question will be endowed with greater mental intensity. I will "see" it better, but I will not see it as if it were *other* than it is, that is to say, as if it were not an individual component of an individual object. The color of this orange will continue to be an individual color, even though I may disregard the other components of the orange [in order to focus on that particular color]. Attention, then, is incapable of transforming a [given sort of] object into another; it does not perform the so-called task of generalization. As proof, I can point to the fact that we can undoubtedly pay attenion to a part or attribute of a concrete object—that we can focus our attention, say, on the color of this orange—precisely insofar as it belongs to this object, this orange, and no other. What is the difference, [then,] between this [kind of] attention which focuses on the individual and that which considers an attribute while disregarding its individuality?

As you can see, this theory does not avoid the implication

that there are acts which are directed—solely and without mediation—to the general as such. The act by which we "understand" the meaning "tree" is qualitatively other than that by which we think of "this tree." The difference lies in the fact that the latter act deals with a representation or image, by means of which, in actual consciousness, the meaning "this tree" is adequately *acknowledged*. The act by which I think of "tree," by contrast, cannot be completely fulfilled by any image. Now, this situation does not hold only for thinking of general entities. When I think, for instance, of "this house," the house I "understand" is intuitively represented by me from one side (which is the only one I see at that point), or from the angle or corner [that two sides of it form]. The three-dimensional house will never *appear*, *in* my *actual* consciousness, exactly and precisely as I think of it; there is always a difference between what I "intend" and what confronts my [particular] mental act of seeing at any given point.

Accordingly, abstraction, regarded as a psychological performance, does not constitute a special problem if we understand the word in terms of its long-standing involvement in the question of how "general ideas" exist in us. Any explanatory psychological theory must acknowledge the ever-present lack of adequate correspondence between what we really or intuitively possess (that which is the *content of our* consciousness) and what expressly constitutes itself as the *object* of our intentive acts. This occurs—except for the case of perceptions and intuitions—in every form of the noetic or intellectual performance of our minds, in every mental act in which we refer to objects as such, i.e., in which we "understand," "mention," or "think of" something.

2: Abstract

THIS PHILOSOPHICAL TERM, which has a precise sense only
in connection with the word "concrete,"[1] has undergone
changes in meaning in every historical period, even though
it refers to a series of problems of primary importance in
logic, psychology, and ontology. Or perhaps it has been
subject to such changes precisely because of that. In some
critical moments of human mental development, this term
did become the main topic of controversy. This was the
case, for example, in Aristotle's dispute with his teacher
Plato concerning the question of whether or not the Platonic
Ideas—the content of which is abstract—in fact have separate existence, apart from concrete things. The most far-
reaching episode of this controversy, which occurred during
the Middle Ages between Nominalists and Realists, was a
repercussion of the classical argument. The age-old conflict
between the proponents of sensualism (or empiricism) and
the advocates of apriorism is, after all, about the nature of
abstraction and the abstract. Such a breach began taking
shape in the seventeenth century in the context of the controversy between Locke and the followers of Descartes, and
it continued in the tradition of English [thought] (e.g., in
[George] Berkeley and [David] Hume), on the one hand,
and in Leibniz and Kant, on the other, until it finally reached
and filled our own era. Under various names, such as psychologism and logicism, positivism and idealism, it has now
reappeared in an aggravated form. Today we can appreciate
the need to deal most carefully with such words, particularly
when we realize that the terms in question, which properly
belong in philosophical discourse, have now come to form
part of the general awareness of the times, thus communi-

cating the seed of fruitful disharmony, potentially contained in them, to the most disparate sectors of culture.

Aristotle was acquainted with the abstract in two senses of the word. First, [we hear him speak of] that which exists separately or by itself (*khoristón*),[2] [what he calls] first substances, i.e., entities like this horse or this man. This is a purely metaphysical sense of "abstract," and only by virtue of a complex network of relationships—which this is not the place to examine—is it connected with the sense of the term under consideration here. Second, [we find him articulating] a purely logical sense, according to which "abstract" refers to the concept resulting when certain elements are mentally removed from a notion. The initial concept would contain a greater number of elements or determinations than the resulting one, and would therefore be concrete, or at least less abstract, in comparison. The content of the abstract concept, then, is the product of the logical operation of "abstraction"—*ta ex areréseos legómena*[3]—and is, so to speak, sustained by and in such an operation. Now *prósthesis*,[4] or the activity of adding [elements] or of progressive determination, is the correlative opposite of abstraction, the logical operation of taking out elements or determinations. As we proceed downward from the generic to the individual concept, the [meanings involved] undergo [increasing] determination, and as we proceed in the opposite direction, they are subjected to abstraction. In the *Nicomachean Ethics*, Aristotle makes very clear what his intention is in establishing the boundary line between the abstract and the concrete by means of the opposition between *diareréseos* and *ex empeirías*, that is to say, between what is obtained by abstraction and what is derived by sense experience. Exactly the same thought appears in the words of [Wilhelm] Wundt which I quote below.

Among the Scholastics, the Nominalists were the ones to introduce in logic the terms "abstract" and "concrete." They employed them especially in connection with names, in which they saw the origin of the duality "abstract vs. concrete," for they believed that it did not exist either in reality or in the conceptual order. On the one hand, every noun, or word used as a noun, is *concrete* if it denotes a particular object or a class of such objects; on the other hand, a name that denotes a property or an attribute is *abstract*. Words like *homo* [man] or *album* [white] are concrete, while those like *humanitas* [humanity] or *albitudo* [whiteness] are abstract.

The sense assigned to these terms began to undergo a transformation during the seventeenth century, when anything not *individual* was regarded as the mere product of our abstractive or generalizing activities. For this reason [John] Locke chose to call those names abstract which express something general. It is in this manner that the individual and the general were confused, respectively, with the concrete and the abstract.

In the nineteenth century, John Stuart Mill returned to the basic Scholastic sense [of the terms], as opposed to the departure represented by Locke. In his *System of Logic*, he speaks of this as follows:

A more wanton alteration in the meaning of a word is rarely to be met with; for the expression *general name*, the exact equivalent of which exists in all languages I am acquainted with, was already available for the purpose to which *abstract* has been misappropriated, while the misappropriation leaves that important class of words, the names of attributes, without any compact distinctive appellation. The old acceptation, however, has not gone so completely out of use, as to deprive those who still adhere to it of all chance of being understood. By *abstract*, then, I shall always mean the opposite of *concrete*: by an abstract noun, the name of an attribute; by a concrete name, the name of an object.[5]

In the eighteenth century, [Christian] Wolff had already concerned himself in his *Logic* with the distinction between the abstract and the general. This is what he said:

Notio abstracta, quae aliquid, quod rei quidam inest re-ladest repraesentat (scilicet rerum attributa, modos, re-lationes) absque ea re, cui inest reladest. (An abstract concept represents something which inherently belongs in a thing, i.e., its attributes, modes, and relations, but it does so without [at the same time] representing the thing in which such inhere.) Notio universalis, qua ea repraesentatur quae rebus plurimis communia sunt. (A universal concept represents something which many things share in common.)[6]

The meaning alteration which originated under the influence of British Empiricism has held fast during the past fifty years, despite the suggestion made by a thinker of Mill's caliber. In one form or another, the intervention—or the failure to intervene—of the functional psychological factor by which we separate elements given together in immediate representation (so as to be able to grasp them by themselves or in isolation) always re-emerges as the principle of the distinction between the abstract and the concrete. As a result, obtaining a precise definition of the terms in question is never possible, since the difference between them—the difference between *what* is abstract and *what* is concrete— is viewed in terms of factors external to the nature of the distinction. Among such external factors are the following: for one, that an abstractive process is instituted in individual consciousness to enable us to think of the abstract; for another, that the quality of being abstract (and, correlatively, that of being concrete) originate on the basis of the comparison between the content of a concept and its psychological representation. This is precisely what Wundt has in mind when he says—albeit recognizing this only as an "extrinsic character"—that in common usage the difference in meaning between such terms lies

in the relationship of the concept to its representational image. We call a concept "concrete" when it is brought to representation not only by means of the word but through a sensuous intuition as well. By contrast, we call it "abstract" when the spoken or written word is the only sign available for the concept. Accordingly, abstract concepts are those to which no *adequate* representation corresponds in our actual consciousness, and for which, therefore, we can find only an external and apparently arbitrary sign in our thinking. In this sense, we characterize as concrete such concepts as *man* or animal, and as abstract those like *humanity* [or animality].[7]

Now [Alois] Höfler carries the psychologistic stance to even greater extremes when he speaks as follows:

To analyze representations consists in finding the *simple* components of a *compound* representation. But how do we carry out the analysis of such representations? In other words, by means of which mental processes do we achieve it? We can *focus* our attention *especially* on the more or less composite elements found in a given representation, and we can focus on one at a time, while *disregarding the rest of the elements*. This psychological process is called "abstracting" or "abstraction," and the representative elements on which [the function of] abstractive attention is focused are referred to as "abstract representations." Finally, those representations which are yet to be subjected to the process of abstraction are known as "concrete." [And, agreeing with Wundt, he adds that] concrete representations can be intuited, while the abstract cannot.[8]

As we have seen, the three authors just quoted refer the terms in question to three different entities: Mill relates them to names, Wundt to concepts, and Höfler to representations. Now, these three entities coincide in that they all are elements of thinking, or psychological constituents of cognition. Apparently, the problem concerning the abstract vs. the concrete is reducible to [the question of] our manner of knowing the abstract and the concrete. The cognitive question involved is a problem of the greatest importance, as we shall have an occasion to see and can now appreciate merely on the grounds of the short terminological history just presented. And yet we shall not be able to deal with this cognitive question with any measure of clarity, unless we have succeeded beforehand in clarifying what the abstract and the concrete are in themselves. Such a task cannot be set aside, even by a theory which comes finally to deny the very existence of the abstract. The judgment "the abstract does not exist" is necessarily based on a prior definition of the nature of the abstract. If such a definition were not available, the judgment in question would be meaningless; it would not be asserting at all what it claims to assert.

In his *Logical Investigations* of [1900–]1901, [Edmund] Husserl has made a significant contribution to the task of clarifying the objective sense of the terms in question. Accordingly, I shall employ his admirable work[9] as the center of reference for all that follows.

The correlation between the abstract and the concrete is just another instance of the relations between *wholes* and *parts*. Every object (be it real, ideal, imaginary, intuitive, or otherwise) either contains parts or is a part of another object. In principle, it is possible for us to classify, on this basis, anything and everything which may become the correlate or terminus of our acts of referring or thinking. In this light, we may say that objects are either parts or wholes. A limb, for example, is a part, or a partial object in the make-up of the whole we term "organic body." Again, a second is part of time, i.e., a numerical unit which is a part of a manifold.

Now then, there are certain objects, the very essence of which renders them incapable of existing unless other specific objects exist as well. Consider the following example. The visual object "color"—and I do not mean here color as understood in physics—intrinsically cannot exist without a perceptible surface to extend upon. (And since I am speaking here of a visual object, to exist means to be perceived.) Color and extension form a whole of which each is a part. And they are non-independent parts, i.e., they cannot be taken out of the whole they constitute. Over against this situation, we can point to the case of the parts into which a line can be divided. Such parts can subsist independently of the whole; when they are no longer parts of the line, they become line segments or points. This finding leads us to another classification: objects are seen to be either independent or non-independent. An object is independent if its existence does not presuppose the co-existence of other objects; an object is non-independent, by contrast, if it is inherently characterized by involvement with other objects in some comprehensive unity, by virtue of having to co-exist with them. It is, therefore, intrinsically a part and only a part of a whole. An instant, or a second, is only what it is *qua* part of the continuum of time.

A non-independent object has usually been defined as one which cannot be *represented by itself*, *in isolation*, or *separately*. An understanding of this sort would, however, affect the very nature of the distinction between independent and non-independent objects. It would no longer be rooted in the very "being" of the objects themselves, since it would have become entirely subjective. In other words, the distinction would be contingent upon our empirical capacity or incapacity to represent an object separately. In this light, we would have to say that a spatial area, which we [in fact] bring to representation as real and separate whenever we open our eyes, would be independent in every sense. But this is not accurate at all, since the spatial area in question is an area—from a geometrical point of view—only if it is delimited by other spatial areas, and the latter would be bounded by still others, and so on and so forth, until we reach the level of infinite, all-encompassing space. By contrast, a living body, of which we cannot *think* except in terms of a milieu where it would perform its living functions, can easily be represented intuitively by itself. To this end, it is enough that it be encompassed by the boundaries of our visual field.

To be sure, for an object to be a member of the sphere of the representable or perceptible, it must conform to the general conditions which constitute that particular sphere. This is also true in the case of the sphere of the mathematical, but the conditions involved here are quite different from those that hold for objects of the perceptible order. No *visible* triangle may be represented without as well bringing to representation its color, while a mathematical triangle has nothing whatsoever to do with that. It is then of fundamental importance never to confuse what is valid for objects essentially belonging in the intuitable domain with what is required for other kinds of objects.

Objects, therefore, are independent or non-independent by virtue of their own [particular] essences, and not because we are subjectively capable or incapable of representing them in isolation.

Now then, the objects which are non-independent parts of a whole, those which require other parts in order to fulfill their own sense, are called abstract parts or objects; they are also referred to as *moments*. [Consider the following.] Intensity and quality are moments or abstract parts of a sound; color and extension are moments or abstract parts of a visible surface. The same holds for the organs of an organism, even though the matter in which such organs are realized can be cut asunder, for only matter *qua* matter, and never the ideal object "organism," can ever be so divided.

By contrast, any object is concrete which does not require another in order to exist. In other words, it is a whole or an independent part.

These are the crucial meanings of the words in question. We may now proceed to employ them in reference to "ideas." When we do so, we find that, in fact, we are unable to perform the act of thinking the generic thought "man," for example, unless we conjoin the intellectual performance or intentive act with some actual content of consciousness, be it the perception of a particular man, or a memory, or a phantasy, or, at least, a verbal image of "man." *Thinking* of the general is a phenomenon of real consciousness which can never be given in isolation, apart from perceiving, imagining, remembering, phantasizing, and so on. It is a *moment*, or abstract part, of our mental reality, just as intensity is an abstract part of sound. And yet who has ever doubted that the intensity of a musical note is itself a reality, different from that of the quality of the sound?

Consequently, [we have to say that] there are no "abstract ideas" in consciousness, but there are *acts* [therein] which render possible the thinking of the "abstract" and the "general" when they are conjoined with other elements.

This series of distinctions is of such importance in pedagogy that it constitutes the very foundation for the education of the intellect. When [Johann H.] Pestalozzi proclaimed the principle of "intuition," he had nothing in mind except the much-bandied-about subject of the abstract and the concrete. And yet the strictly pedagogical application of the clear notion of the abstract can only be effected when the questions of conceptualization and thinking are dealt with in their entirety.

3: Apperception

In one form or another, the doctrine of apperception constitutes the very core of psychology. Hence, the slightest variation in the point of view we may adopt in considering the mental sphere will bring about a new and distinctive theoretical account of apperception. The history of this term is therefore most eventful. In fact, subjects vastly different from each other have been referred to by this term at one time or another. Any attempt to reconstruct the self-identical sense which lies hidden in such a multiplicity of meanings would require us systematically to study the entire history of modern philosophy.

In attempting to present this doctrine, then, the only avenue open to us is that of a quick review of the major vicissitudes in the history of the concept of apperception. In this review, I shall try to indicate the conceptual progress made in each of the critical moments involved. A problem undergoes evolution very much as an organism does: its successive manifestations are so many stages in the progressive unfolding of one and the same problem structure. In fact, the series of answers proposed for it is made up of the relative solutions corresponding to the particular stages the problem has gone through. Having been resolved according to one of the ways in which it was posed, the problem reappears in a more precise, condensed, and concise form. In this light, [we can say that] the advancement of science is evinced more accurately by the greater precision and exactitude achieved in the formulation of its problems than by the adequacy of the solutions proposed for them.

Let us begin with an example from our mental life. The instance is, strictly speaking, typical, since we always find our actual consciousness to be constituted by, or to be concerned with, this particular phenomenon, no matter when we observe ourselves. Let us say that I now see a cup in front of me. The cup I *am referring* to is thought by me to be a real "object," an object actually existing in space. This characterization of the cup is applicable as well to many other objects, some of which I now see (or believe I see), while others I only imagine or remember or simply think about. It is evident that since the cup is located in space, it is not found in my consciousness; it is not a part thereof. The situation, formulated exactly by the expression "I see a cup," consists in my realization that two objects different from one another co-exist, constituting the boundaries of one another. I mean here the objects known as "cup" and "I." [The situation] will become altogether different the moment I stop looking at the cup (i.e., the very instant I cease to focus my attention merely on the cup) and instead look at the situation itself (i.e., my "seeing of the cup"). In that case, the "object" I am confronted with is no longer the material "cup," which is located in space, but the immaterial thing I may call "my visual experience of the cup," or my own act of consciousness. At this point, whether the cup truly exists or is just a hallucination is no concern of mine, for, in the new situation, I am busy not with the cup but only with my "visual experience" of it. I said before that the first situation could be understood as the confrontation of two objects, namely, "cup" and "I." In the new situation the confrontation will occur between two other objects, namely, "I" who have come to the realization of having seen the cup, and another "I," precisely the "I" who was seeing the cup when the first situation was still in effect.

Is it perchance strange to regard a "visual experience of the cup" and "I" as one and the same thing? If we think that, then we should attempt to determine the nature of what I call "I" in the first situation. Or to put it differently:

we should try to establish the nature of what is posited by the ego, as well as by the cup, to produce—as the net result—my visual experience of the cup. If we do that, we shall discover, soon enough, that the cup is, say, in the shape of a cylinder, or that it approximates that of a cone. In other words, we shall find that it is a three-dimensional object, exhibiting various "sides" or "faces." Now then, when I am engaged in seeing a cup, I see, strictly speaking, only one side, or, if you will, a cup endowed with only one face and, therefore, a cup which is no cup at all. Coming to realize this is crucial, since it shows us that the "object" known as "cup" has split into two quite different things: the real cup which does not confront us at all, and the visual configuration, endowed with color and determinate shape, which does confront us but is no cup at all. If we change our position, or if we move away, the colored shape [accordingly] changes, and yet we still believe ourselves to be seeing the same invariable cup, even as the colored shape alters its appearance. Now then, such shapes or images are but *our* successive *ways of being conscious* of one and the same object. They are what we or the ego posit, and, as such, they are merely parts of the ego. The cup will always be beyond them, and we shall always see the cup *by means of* them, i.e., *in* our own *perceptions*.

Now, the consequence of this is as simple as it is instructive. The sentence "I see a cup" is ambiguous. What I see, what is part and parcel of my visual experience, is an inadequate, imprecise image of the cup, presenting it from only one side. But this is [the result of] no error or illusion. On the contrary, it is [due to] the very nature of consciousness itself. I am conscious of the cup, which I do not actually see, but I am not conscious of what is *actually found* in my visual experience, i.e., the image [of the cup]. Perception (i.e., what is usually termed "seeing") breaks down, then, into two very different components: the act of seeing—strictly speaking—an image, and the act of interpreting the image (i.e., what is present in me) as an *image of* a real cup.

From this we could derive several points of fundamental importance for the whole field of psychology. But our subject here forces us to bear in mind only those which are strictly necessary to clarify the meaning of the term "apperception."

As I have just pointed out, perception, which seems to be the simplest form of consciousness, involves [in fact] two different and simpler forms of awareness, namely, pure "vision" (or visual experience proper), and the act of interpreting the latter (or what is [actually] seen) as the stand-in for the object. Perception is the resultant of both mental performances. In this resultant, however, a favored status is enjoyed by the second [component] performance—the one which is directed to, and by virtue of which we are conscious of, the object. By contrast, pure "vision" goes unnoticed in perception, for we are not conscious of the fact that we see a caricature or [partial] image of the cup. To come to this discovery, we had to transform the original situation (in which we found ourselves engaged when we were seeing the cup) into an object of analysis. We had to step out of our perceptual involvement and place ourselves before the latter, as if it were a thing. Now, "reflection" has [traditionally] been the name given to this new placement of the ego with respect to an object which is a part of the ego[1] and also an "ego" itself. By reflection, then, we have discovered that in the typical case in question, consciousness is invariably constituted by elements of two sorts, namely, those which we are not conscious of, and those which we are conscious of. And for our purposes, the typical case [of the perception of the cup] validly represents any other we could choose. In our case, pure "vision" actually provides unnoticed support for the act of objective interpretation. We have unquestionably identified here two different degrees of consciousness. Or to put it otherwise: being conscious is only a relative quality, for, had we never seen the image, we would never have perceived the presence of the object (in this example, the cup). Seeing should then be regarded not as a failure at becoming conscious, but rather as the minimal degree of consciousness, as opposed to the act of adverting to an object, which is in this case the performance characterized by the maximum degree of consciousness.

Leibniz[2] came to the conclusion that the act of consciousness by which we become aware of the roar of the sea latently contains those events by which we grasp the noise made by each [component] wave, and he did so on remarking that the [hearing of the] roar of the sea derives—physiologically speaking—from the minimal stimulations proceeding from each separate wave. We must have heard the minute noises, [or so the argument goes,] since we hear the total noise they constitute, and yet we hear minute and total noises in different degrees. We are conscious of the fact that we hear the total noise, but we hear the component noises without yet being conscious of them. Leibniz called the merely heard noises *petites perceptions*, and he used the term "apperception" to refer to our consciousness of hearing, or to our hearing of hearing, as it were. Thus we find—in one stroke—both the historical and the rational origins of the term.

By way of Kant and [Johann F.] Herbart, Leibniz's distinction between "perception" and "apperception" has become part of contemporary psychology. It must be said, however, that the ambiguities besetting Leibniz's employment of these expressions have not yet been completely removed.

On the one hand, it seems inconsistent to refer to such events as *petites perceptions*, since "perception" means perceiving some content or other, and yet the perceptual content is not supposed to exist for consciousness [in such cases].

Leibniz was no doubt pointing by the name "perception" to a would-be law, according to which a perception would become "*apperceptible* by a little addition or increase."[3] This certainly holds true for many contents of consciousness of which we are not conscious at a given point, but may become conscious at another. But the fact remains that there are many contents or constituents of consciousness of which we can never become apperceptively conscious. These are the "sensations" without which apperception would be altogether impossible. Consequently, the difference between perception and apperception cannot be simply one of degree, which could be overcome by mere increase or addition. If, to go back to the previous example, we were to attempt to resolve the image of the cup, in turn, into partial images, we would [eventually] realize that we never attain the situation of consciousness in which the duality between what is merely sensed and what is perceived is abolished. "Sensing" and "perceiving" are two irreducible forms of consciousness.

On the other hand, "apperception" has a twofold sense, even in Leibniz. Above I characterized the experience he discusses as becoming "conscious of the fact that we hear," or as "our hearing of hearing." Now this may have two different meanings. First, it may signify the fact of becoming conscious of the sense we have when the ego is faced with *something* not immediately itself, indeed with that which is other than "ego" or "subject," namely, an "object." Second, it may also denote the event in which the ego places before itself, as an object, something which is part of itself. This second sense would be the equivalent of "self-consciousness." As defined by Leibniz elsewhere, apperception would thus be "consciousness or the reflective knowledge of this inner state [or perception] itself . . . which is not given to all souls [e.g., to animals] or to any soul all the time."[4]

Apperception would accordingly be the special prerogative of the human psyche.

If we reflect a moment on the twofold meaning of the term, we shall not fail to notice, on the one hand, that apperception is—in view of the first sense of the word—a special *form* of consciousness, the distinctive characteristics of which become available if we compare it with another special *form* of consciousness, i.e., perception (which, in the terminology we have adopted here, would be called sensation). On the other hand, if we introduce a qualification in the meaning of the term, we obtain its second sense. We do so by connecting apperception with a *special sort of content* [of consciousness], namely, with inner states. As we can see, the two senses of the term belong in two different orders of classification.

Now, from a purely descriptive standpoint, from the point of view of classification, it will no doubt prove most convenient to keep to the first sense of "apperception." We certainly enjoy the consciousness of having engaged in a relationship with an "object," i.e., of being presented with something exhibiting independence, a feature which is at once irreducible and ultimate on the one hand and clear and precise on the other. By contrast, we also find in ourselves another form of awareness, radically different from the former in that its content is experienced not as external to consciousness but as an inner state. Such a content remains part of our actual ego, and we cannot therefore advert to it as if it were something independent of us. Even the smallest perceptible part of the black shade of color extending on this table is no longer, from this point of view, a color sensation of *mine*, but the *objectivation* of my sensation, or its transformation into an object. The sensation is mine; it is [part of the] ego. But the black color *belongs* to the table, and is located in space.

Let us then agree to abide strictly by the following definitions of the terms in question. By "apperception," we shall signify that kind of content of consciousness in which we encounter an object as such, and by "sensation" (the "perception" of Leibniz, Kant, Herbart, and many of our contemporaries) that kind of content of consciousness which never acquires the status of an object. We may correlate these definitions, which are formulated in terms of content of consciousness, with others that are derived when consciousness is considered from the point of view of activity. In this light, we can define "apperception" as the act of referring to an "object" as such, and "sensation" as that component of consciousness which is its non-actual matter and [therefore] no act of any kind.

Any connection between this descriptive sense of apperception and Leibniz's second meaning of the term ("self-consciousness") may be clearly grasped at once if we consider Kant's theory of apperception.

Now, moving in this direction is by no means easy. Leibniz's point of departure, in all we have said above, is the simple fact of observing a real phenomenon of consciousness. We recognize that this is the case with Leibniz, even as we identify in him a tendency to solve the same sort of problems as Kant, and even when we see him resolving them in a manner very much like Kant's. Leibniz's concept of apperception is developed on the basis of definite psychological evidence. Only when he has formulated the concept in psychological terms does he employ it as a logical principle. Kant, however, is concerned only with the problem of logical consciousness, or cognition. But cognition is definable in terms of values, not facts. Cognition involves a claim to truth, for its object is something quite different from what we referred to above as "object" (e.g., the cup). The object of cognition is the true as such. But, according to Kant, the true is not anything which simply is, in the ordinary sense of the word "being"; rather, the true is that which *has to be* as it is, and cannot be otherwise. To begin with, Kant is not concerned with determining whether there is in fact an intellectual function capable of grasping the supreme object called truth, here on earth, or on any other planet for that matter. Rather, his task is to identify what the structure intrinsically belonging to the activity of thinking must be, if it is validly to lay claim to being an act of cognition in the sense just indicated. The problem he deals with is not proper to the realm of empirical observation, but rather a matter of purely rational construction, very much in the sense we give to this term in connection with a mathematical problem. We proceed in this manner when we ask, for example, about the nature of a triangle which would meet a specific requirement, say, that the square on the side subtending a right angle be equal to the squares on the sides containing the right angle.

If we reduce Kant's reasoning to its essentials, we see that it could not possibly exhibit greater clarity or firmness. A judgment, or the particular content of a cognition, is universal and necessary, he would argue, if and only if what it affirms or denies about things has to do exclusively with the conditions to be fulfilled by anything, if it is to be present to us as a cognitive problem.

Let us consider an example, even if to do so we must provisionally come down from the purely logical plane on which Kant is moving. To be able to formulate a true or a false judgment, I must first establish a relationship with the thing I shall be referring to by the judgment in question, or with the thing which the judgment will express. Let the judgment be, for instance, the assertion that the sum of the internal angles of a plane triangle equals two right angles. This judgment lays claim on the truth, for the content affirmed is meant to be valid for all the triangles I have seen and for all those which are possible. Now, how can anyone venture to make an assertion like this, (in an a priori manner or) *before* even considering each and every triangle? We may say, to begin with, that a triangle is an area of [two-dimensional] space which is enclosed by three [straight] lines. In turn, each such line is a manifold composed of points. But I ask: How is it possible for my consciousness to *contain* such a manifold?

[For this to be possible, three requirements] must be met. *First of all*, I must be able to run successively through each and every point therein, whether the points be finite or infinite in number, and then I must be able to put them together as a manifold. If not, the points will not be in my consciousness. ([This is what Kant calls the] Synthesis of Apprehension in Intuition.)[5] *Second*, for this to *be possible*, it is also *necessary* that I retain my [consciousness of] the first point simultaneously with my consciousness of the second, [and the equivalent must hold in the case of the third,] and so on and so forth. My *actual* consciousness of a *further* point requires the presence at the same time of my reproductive consciousness or memory of the *one* point [coming before], for otherwise I would never be able to abandon that one and only point, and the line would [consequently] never be [produced or generated]. ([This is what Kant calls the] Synthesis of Reproduction in Imagination.)[6] *Third*, to be able to gather [at once] in *one* consciousness the actual *further* point and the *one* point now remembered, I must—justifiably—be capable of recognizing the latter as the same point I held in my mind a moment earlier. Now, some vague act of identification will never do. [In other words, we] need an act of identification proper, which can only be effected by means of a *concept* already available to us. Such a concept would be used by us "as a rule" in distinguishing and exactly determining any component of my representation (in this case, the point I am now remembering). For me to be able to re-cognize the *first* point, and the *second*, and the *third*, [and so on,] and to identify them as such, I must have at my disposal the notion of time, which is an order of placement, or a distributive assignment in terms of "before" and "after." ([This is what Kant calls the] Synthesis of Recognition in a Concept.)[7]

Nothing may thus become an object for me unless I gather in one consciousness the sequence of acts of consciousness in which the elements of the object are given to me. Or to put if differently: all successive acts of consciousness must be *mine*; the self-identical consciousness of the ego must run through every one of them. In Kant's own words, it "must be possible for the 'I think' to accompany all my representations,"[8] simply because otherwise they would not be mine. Now then, every representation, perception, or sensation is different from the rest by virtue of its own [particular] content. If receptivity were the only capacity present in me—and this is precisely the assumption made by both realism and positivism—then every instant in [the life of] consciousness would be entirely self-enclosed; I would be born and I would die with every new instant. If this were so, I would be reducible to a [mere] sequence of momentary egos which would remain alien to each other, and I would possess only pointlike contents, devoid of any possible meaning. In brief, I would possess nothing at all. The transition from one act of consciousness to another, subject to the condition that the latter be recognized as a continuation of the former, or as a part of the same ego which existed the moment before, requires that the ego be active rather than passive, or that it consist in carrying out the same, self-identical performance at every turn. Kant refers to this active function of the ego as "apperception." The ego has a consciousness of its own identity, because it is a unity of apperception. This unity of apperception is a system formed by spontaneous intellectual functions, which interpret or elaborate the sensuous material by transforming it into a conceptual network, that is to say, into a full-fledged consciousness. The categories (e.g., unity, plurality, substance, and causality) are the functions which weave sensations (the unconscious factors of consciousness) into one another, thus rendering possible the [form of] consciousness in which the ego does not sense an object but thinks it. (Cf. *Kant*.)[9]

This forced and extremely brief outline shows that Kant's notion of apperception turns out to be an *ideal* mechanism rationally required to explain Leibniz's first sense of the term, namely, that of becoming conscious of an object *qua* object.

With Kant (although in this, to be sure, he had been anticipated by Leibniz), we reach a turning point in the history of the old-style psychology, which is thereby replaced by a science based on the notion of activity. At this juncture, Herbart proceeds to transfer Kant's logical construction to the plane of the empirical scientific study of the phenomena of consciousness. In the field of pedagogy, his theoretical account of apperception is of monumental importance. (Cf. *Herbart*.)[10]

Let us limit ourselves here to a few words about it.

Herbart begins with the assumption that the soul is a simple substance, engaged in self-transcending relationships with other simple substances, both material and spiritual. The qualitatively simple character of the soul is the principle ruling all its vicissitudes. Now, since simplicity is unity, mental life turns out to be nothing but the struggle to secure unity, in opposition to the heterogeneous [influences] exerted on the soul by other substances.

Let A be the soul, and let S be another substance colliding with it. A would respond to such an event (*perturbación*) by means of what Herbart calls an act of *self-preservation*, by virtue of which the entire soul would become endowed with a specific quality and character. Such acts of self-preservation Herbart calls sensations. Now, some such events are identical to [each other], others are just similar, and still others are quite different. This is due to the fact that the events in question have different origins, some having their source in kindred substances, some in less similar ones. Now, A has responded to [the influence of] S by means of sensation a, but the simplicity of A does not then allow [the soul] to respond by means of sensation b to [the influence of] another substance, S', which is quite different from S. As a consequence, a conflict will arise between b and a, i.e., between the [result of the] new stimulation and the sensation which [already] constitutes the actual state of the soul or conscious substance. In such a struggle, sensation a will first become *obstructed* or *impeded* (*estorbada*), and will then *combine* (*complicar*) itself with sensation b (or fuse with it if b is a kindred sensation, such as one belonging in the same qualitative order—say, color or sound). The *combination* formed by a and b constitutes a new unit, for it is not tantamount to the simple co-existence of a and b. Combinations and fusions are second-degree states [of the soul]. They are the more complex conditions called representations. We observe the same mechanical forces at work among the latter as among the initial sensations. In other words, a new representation will succeed in crossing the *threshold of consciousness*, or will come to awareness, only if representations already in the soul assimilate it by transforming and interpreting it in their image and likeness. This is precisely the process involved in apperception. Nothing may gain access to consciousness if there is a breach of continuity between itself and what already exists in consciousness. To become conscious of something, to allow the new to reach awareness, will then amount to enveloping and permeating it with the old. Only in this fashion will the ultimate and essential character of consciousness (i.e., its unity or identity) be preserved.

One can easily appreciate how fruitful are the guidelines

made available by this theory—which is not as true as it is simple and keen—to the science of pedagogy, which is concerned precisely with the question of how a child's consciousness may gain access to what it does not already contain. Past and present representations are the means to be used in apperception, and the new is whatever is to be apperceived. Mental life is thus seen as subject to the operation of a rather simple mechancial process, to which Herbart aspired to give mathematical expression.

[Wilhelm] Wundt would reap no small harvest on the basis of Herbart's psychological account, although he came to differ radically from Herbart's position. Herbart reduces mental life to its representational or intellectual aspects, but Wundt places the affective dimension, or voluntary activity, at the center of his concept of apperception, and takes such a dimension or activity to be the very axis around which consciousness revolves. In fact, he construes voluntary activity as the moving force in the stream of mental life. For this reason his doctrine is known as *apperceptive and voluntaristic psychology*, and is viewed as being in opposition to the intellectualism characteristic of *associationistic psychology*.

This notwithstanding, we must state that the distinctive concern with precision which is manifest in the work of Leibniz, Kant, and Herbart does not find an echo in Wundt, who is more of an experimenter than a philosopher. His concept of apperception is a confused and manifold notion, formed by several components having little to do with each other, as we are about to see.

According to Wundt, consciousness seems to consist of strands of various sorts. First of all, we have the simple sensations, the ultimate materials of the mind. Although these are not actually given in real consciousness, the work of abstraction carried out by the investigator can reveal them as the essential stuff of which it is composed. [Consider an example.] A simple sound is a sensation. We always hear it in conjunction with others and inseparably joined to representations, memories, local and temporal determinations, feelings, and so on. Now, for our purposes, let us focus on the representational phases, to the exclusion of the affective ones. [In this context, Wundt would have to say that] *mental structures* arise as a result of the *fusion* of sensations. According to him, a mental structure is "any compound content of our immediate experience that stands out among the rest by virtue of specific features, thus appearing as a relatively independent unit, to which we may assign a special name whenever such is practically required." Mental structures are characterized by the fact that their properties "can never be completely resolved into those proper to the mental elements of which they are composed." They constitute something new. The mental structures identifiable in the intellectual sphere are *representations*. Despite the fact that they are something new, representations are not still other sensations, not even complex ones (a contention which, in any case, would involve a self-contradiction), but rather "special *forms for the ordering of sensations*."[11] Among the representations, we find the "intensive" ones, such as those of space and time.

Mental structures or formations do not—like sensations—arise as a result of abstraction. They are real units encountered in real consciousness. We can find and discern them within the field produced by real consciousness itself. In fact, they are justifiably characterized as contents *of* consciousness. Now consciousness [as such] is the third, full-fledged phase [of this totality]. Representations dwell either simultaneously or successively, thus forming [constituent] threads of a fabric, together with compound feelings and volitions. The resulting texture is consciousness. To become conscious of something is to have the corresponding phenomenon appear within the "visual field of consciousness." Such a phenomenon, however, does not arise in isolation;

rather it forms a tissue with others and—in conjunction with them—becomes part of an [encompassing] perspectival arrangement. Now then, the act of becoming conscious can be more or less *clear and distinct*. The maximum degree of clarity is like a center of mental brightness within the field of consciousness. A special "sense of activity" is always a concomitant of that center of clarity. It seems to us as if we ourselves raised up, underscored, and placed emphasis on the favored content, i.e., as if we were addressing ourselves to it or were focusing on it. Such a phenomenon is called attention.

Hence there are always elements-not-attended-to *and* elements-attended-to in the field of consciousness. According to Wundt, the former are mere perceptions, and the latter apperceptions. The difference between them—contends the Leipzig psychologist—is not qualitative; it is rather a matter of degree. Apperception is sometimes accompanied by attention, but may be either *passive* or *active*, a passion being an example of apperception not accompanied by attention.

Apperception is, according to Wundt, the *process* by which a mental content is clarified. It is therefore nothing but a name for the extremely complex system of conditions which *explanatory* psychology must study if it is to understand the state of consciousness at any given moment.

The circular path that the term "apperception" has traversed in this exposition is now completely before our eyes. First of all, we determined it to be a characteristic exhibited by consciousness at every juncture. This was the descriptive concept of apperception. But eventually it turned out to be the expression of the genetic or causal conditions of the state of consciousness in question. Precisely here lies the difference between descriptive and explanatory psychology, which can be clearly grasped in this particular case. When we look for the cause of something, we must go beyond the limits of descriptive analysis, even if we happen to establish that the components of the cause in question are not hypothetical (as in physics) but real, and can be described one by one.

Perhaps we could interpret Wundt's position by saying that, at every turn, consciousness constitutes itself as an integral unity. At any given moment, the state of consciousness, or the particular content emerging, depends on the unity of consciousness prevailing at the instant before. By the name "apperception," Wundt seeks to give expression to the connection between every real phenomenon of consciousness and the previous state of consciousness, namely, that condition in the light of which the appearance of the phenomenon in question may become intelligible. Accordingly, if we judge by the function to be performed, apperception as understood by Wundt is no different from apperception as conceived by Herbart. It would be no great mistake, then, to assert that apperception plays in Wundt's psychological theory the same role as energy in contemporary physics.

Now then, the newly emerging content may arise without that sense of activity we called attention being clearly identifiable in the state of consciousness preceding it. This would signify that apperception has taken place [so to speak] underground, or at least that we cannot ascertain in our consciousness [the presence of a sense of] responsibility for the new content. When this occurs, we have to say that apperception is functioning passively.

Association is the process involved in passive apperception. Elements fuse thereby with one another; they combine; they assimilate one another; they reproduce themselves, so to speak. [This is the phenomenon of] memory. All of this seems to occur simultaneously. The resulting contents constitute only the zone of consciousness which we do not advert to. This will suffice for the moment, since the study of such contents properly and conveniently belongs under the heading "Association."[12]

Another case would involve those contents which "are immediately produced under the influence of attention." The processes by which such contents are generated are known in common experience under the names "thinking," "reflection," "phantasy," or "intelligence." They constitute the higher-level activity of the mind.

As we can see, such processes are characterized by the role played in them by attention. According to Wundt's analysis, attention is reducible to the very constituents of voluntary action. (Cf. "Will".)[13] He does introduce one qualification, however; according to him, the will is directed [in the case in point] to representational contents. Now then, full-fledged voluntary action is the culmination of a mental process in which the totality of consciousness, at a given moment, is gathered and concentrated most vigorously and closely. The ego is precisely the sense or consciousness of such unity. Here originates the evidence by which we recognize ourselves as the source of our actions. In voluntary action, we set the awareness we have of ourselves *as subjects* over against whatever may be playing the role of correlate or terminus of consciousness. By means of this disjunction, the latter appears as that which is confronting the ego, i.e., as the non-ego or "object." (Please note that the second sense of Leibniz's concept of apperception reappears here, in conjunction with Kant's notion of "transcendental apperception," and together with what Wundt has adopted from Herbart's doctrine.)

By operating in this way, attention endows the content of consciousness with the objectivity, independence, or transcendence to which I referred in the opening section of this entry.

The succession of representations—their connection and combination—is subject in apperception to a voluntary process. We pick out images and place them at the inner center of brightness or luminosity; we set others aside; or we pull them to pieces and keep some of their elements, which we then join to other elements, until we manage to build total representations; and so on and so forth.

The most interesting thing about active apperception is that it always operates on contents it finds already preformed by passive apperception. The tasks it performs are second-degree functions; the products it generates have many constituents.

Wundt divides such functions into simple and compound. The simple are those which establish *relations* and *comparisons*. (Comparing is a special operation within the wider or more general function of relating, since comparing consists in relating two terms in the particular respect of their equality or inequality.) The compound are functions like synthesis and "analysis." On the basis of analysis arise even more concrete functions, for example, phantasy "and the understanding." Every one of these terms could give rise to much doubt and provoke many a discussion, but they would all pertain to particular questions which are out of place in a general entry on apperception such as this one.

Now this will suffice. Here I have just presented—concisely and by way of outline—what I would call the classical doctrine of apperception. Any exposition contained in a dictionary should be limited to this, since a work of this sort has no room for the discussions actually taking place in the living science of the day. These would concern subjects so fundamental that they require a more detailed examination, which can only be engaged in at the risk of having the reader lose his way. I cannot bring this essay to an end, however, without remarking that the basic problems of psychology are at present undergoing such profound changes that no one interested in this science can evade the responsibility for correcting the classical doctrines of the discipline, by means of reforms which have been proposed most recently.

[A NOTE ON] PEDAGOGY

We have seen that apperception is the essential moving force of consciousness, or the very center of its self-creation. And this is so even for an advocate of physiological psychology, such as Wundt. Apperception is anything that lies beyond the sensuous, which is just dead product and mere material for the mental life. Pedagogy may no doubt therefore conclude that it should regard itself, on the whole, as a discipline based on apperception. The vast scope of this subject clearly transcends any limits we could impose on it; hence this is not the proper place to deal with the wealth of pedagogical problems encompassed under the heading "apperception."

To begin with, we find that attention is a component of apperception. Now then, a significant part of classical pedagogy—especially Herbart's—is devoted to educational questions pertinent to attention. This is accomplished under the name "interest." We shall examine such matters in that entry.[14]

Nevertheless, we must address ourselves to the most general problem in the field of pedagogy, since the apperceptive function is of decisive importance. We have seen that apperception, according to Kant, Herbart, and Wundt, involves the question of the genesis of consciousness [as such], or the development of a state of consciousness out of a previous phase of the conscious life. Parallel to this psychological problem, we find in pedagogy another of comparable importance, namely, the question of the proper sequence of stages to be observed in education. The way to teach a particular subject is a special matter, to be dealt with in the methodology or didactics proper to the field of study in point. This is also the case concerning the manner of educating feeling and the will. But determining the temporal order of pedagogical interventions is a problem which demands prior study and resolution.

Now the order to be followed in structuring the educational process is far from obvious. For example, we still hear people talk, as if it were a deep and illuminating truth, of the coincidence between the evolution of the human individual and that of mankind. (In fact, Baldwin[15] attempted to bring back this view in a book published not long ago.) The coarse materialism that ruled over Europe thirty years ago and kept it most content and at ease with the discovery of the biogenetic law believed the validity of this principle could be extended from the biological to the spiritual realm. [On that basis,] a not very sensible pedagogical theory promulgated the notion that educational subjects should be presented to the child in the same order in which the human race had experienced and created them. Accordingly, since man began by seeing the world in terms of a mythical form of apperception, the child was to be acquainted first of all with mythical-religious stories and fairy tales. In the sphere of the will, Zeller,[16] a famous follower of Herbart, established six levels or degrees of [human] moral evolution, which he proposed to spread through the eight grades of schooling.

Capesius,[17] for one, most sensibly points out that there is no necessary correspondence between the historical process and the sequence to be followed in school. So he says:

The science of logic, for example, was established in history long before we succeeded in scientifically explaining the simplest natural phenomena. This fact notwithstanding, we have to teach in school about Galileo's discoveries before we attempt to present the doctrines of Aristotle. The theory of electricity is almost entirely a product of our times. The fact that lightning and an electrical spark are identical was ascertained only toward the middle of the eighteenth century. Again, the first electromagnetic phenomena were discovered during the first twenty years of the nineteenth century. And yet we shall teach our students about the identity of lightning and the electrical spark and about the general facts in the area of electromagnetic phenomena before we try to acquaint them with the laws governing central motion, which were already established by Huyghens in 1633.[18]

Notes

1. To the first edition of *Psychological Investigations: Investigaciones psicológicas*, in *Obras de José Ortega y Gasset* (Madrid: Alianza Editorial, 1982).

2. As *Investigaciones psicológicas* has now become part of volume XII of the *Obras Completas* of Ortega [Centenary Edition (Madrid: Alianza Editorial/Revista de Occidente, 1983)], I have excluded the second essay, which is found in volume I [pp. 244ff.] of the set. [This essay is "Sobre el concepto de sensación"; the English version appears as "On the Concept of Sensation," in José Ortega y Gasset, *Phenomenology and Art*, trans. P. W. Silver (New York: W. W. Norton & Company, 1975), pp. 95ff. The first essay, "Sensación, construcción e intuición," also appears in this edition of the *Obras Completas* (XII, pp. 487ff.); the English version, "Sensation, Construction, and Intuition," is to be found in *Phenomenology and Art*, pp. 79ff. In this edition of *Psychological Investigations* I am therefore excluding both pieces, since they are already available in English.—TRANS.]

ONE

1. In the Spanish edition of this work, every lecture is preceded by a summary of its contents, in brackets, supplied by the editor. I have kept the summaries, but dropped the brackets. —TRANS.

2. Apparently only this course of fifteen lectures was given, out of the proposed series.—TRANS.

3. *De divisione naturae*, I, p. 71.

TWO

1. Instead of "color of the body" (*color del cuerpo*), the passage reads "bodily heat" (*calor del cuerpo*), which does not make sense in the context, particularly in the last sentence of the paragraph.—TRANS.
2. I presume that Ortega means by "summary" the results of the endeavor of which these pages are the first draft, and by "fuller exposition" possibly a book he had planned to write on the basis of this lecture series.—ED.

THREE

1. Ortega employs "science" to refer to any systematic study, whether empirical or not. As a first approximation, we could say that for him noology is the theory of sense in general, as opposed and prior to truth (cf. lecture 12, p. 163); ontology is the theory of being, or of the object (cf. lecture 1, p. 35); semiology, or general grammar, is the theory of the essential features of language (cf. lecture 1, p. 35, lecture 8, p. 132, and lecture 15, pp. 187–88); and logic is the theory of truth (cf. table, p. 202, which includes all four of the terms in question). —TRANS.
2. "Mathematics as a Cultural Function," January 31, 1914. —ED.
3. Cf. Aristotle, *Metaphysics*, 1003a.—TRANS.

FIVE

1. Here we may read the text to say "by means of," or perhaps "in," but not "is" (*es*) as the original inconsistently has it. —TRANS.
2. The following four paragraphs constitute the only part of this course published before. They appeared in volume I of *El Espectador*.—ED. [Cf. Editor's Preface, p. 23. I have translated this section directly from the original even though it has already appeared in English as part of "Consciousness, the Object, and Its Three Distances," in *Phenomenology and Art*, pp.

116–19, so as to ensure unity of style and greater closeness to the text. I have of course kept the previous version in mind. —Trans.]

3. Instead of "being" (*ser*), the passage reads "seeing" (*ver*), which does not make sense in the context.—Trans.

4. Cf. Edmund Husserl, *Ideas Pertaining to a Pure Phenomenology and to a Phenomenological Philosophy*, I, § 94.—Trans.

5. The following paragraphs appear to constitute a draft for a commentary on the table appearing between lectures 4 and 5, [now in appendix, p. 202].—Ed.

6. This interpolation is by the editor.—Trans.

SIX

1. Cf. Aristotle, *On the Soul*, 432a.—Trans.

2. René Descartes, *Meditations on the First Philosophy*, ii.—Trans.

3. Cf. Aristotle, *Metaphysics*, 983–84; *Categories*, 2a14–4b19. —Trans.

SEVEN

1. Ortega's sense is clear, but he transposes the order in the proportion, for he presents it as "scientific language is to everyday language as pragmatic things are to theoretical objects." I have corrected this in the translation.—Trans.

2. I have been unable to identify this author.—Trans.

3. I have been unable to identify the original of this quote, which has therefore been translated directly from Ortega's Spanish version.—Trans.

4. Aristotle, *Metaphysics*, 1074b.—Trans.

5. Except for the last two paragraphs, the rest of this lecture is identical with the second fragment of the course which was published as part of *El Espectador*.—Ed. [Cf. Editor's Preface, p. 23. As in lecture 5, rather than using the available English version (part of "Consciousness, the Object, and Its Three Distances," in *Phenomenology and Art*, pp. 119–24), I have translated this section directly from the original.—Trans.]

6. Cf. Miguel de Cervantes, *The History of Don Quixote de la Mancha*, Part I, ch. 4.—TRANS.

7. Obviously, the passage in brackets was omitted by mistake, since it appears in the fragment of the lecture which was originally published in *El Espectador*. Without it, the important conceptual distinction Ortega has elaborated here would be inexact or remain incomplete. Cf. Editor's Preface, p. 23. —TRANS.

8. Cf. Edmund Husserl, *Logical Investigations*, trans. J. N. Findlay (New York: The Humanities Press, 1970), I, pp. 280–81.—TRANS.

9. Ortega's parenthetical remark shows how interested he was in preserving the text of this lecture series.—ED.

EIGHT

1. Instead of "causality" (*causalidad*), the passage reads "chance" (*casualidad*), which does not seem to make sense in the context.—TRANS.

2. Cf. [Heinrich] Maier, *Psychologie des emotionales Denkens*, 1908, p. 143.

3. Let us set the phenomena of dividing aside, for, in the final analysis, dividing is a modality of joining or combining. [This parenthetical remark was originally part of the text.—TRANS.]

4. Lask was one of the members of the new generation of most promising [German] professors; he died just a few months ago on the battlefield. [This parenthetical remark was originally part of the text.—TRANS.]

5. Cf. Husserl, *Logical Investigations*, II, pp. 553ff.—TRANS.

6. I have been unable to identify the original of this quote, which has therefore been translated directly from Ortega's Spanish version.—TRANS.

7. Ortega may be speaking of the logical necessity of "2 + 2 = 4."—TRANS.

NINE

1. Cf. George Berkeley, *A Treatise concerning the Principles of Human Knowledge*, §3.—TRANS.

TEN

1. Plato, *Apology*, 38a.—TRANS.
2. I have been unable to identify the original of this quote, which has therefore been translated directly from Ortega's Spanish version.—TRANS.
3. Cf. Plato, *Phaedo*, 76b.—TRANS.
4. Cf. Descartes, *Meditations*, i.—TRANS.
5. Agrippa is quoted in Sextus Empiricus, *Outlines of Pyrrhonism*, I.—TRANS.
6. Ibid.—TRANS.
7. Cf. Plato, *Theaetetus*, 152a.—TRANS.
8. For the significance of this point, see lecture 12, p. 175. The reference is to Cervantes, *Don Quixote*, Part I, ch. 21 and 25. —TRANS.
9. This phrase is in English in the original, but Hume does not seem to use it; rather, he employs "customary conjunction." Cf. David Hume, *An Enquiry concerning Human Understanding*, V, Part I.—TRANS.
10. Friedrich Nietzsche, *Werke*, ed. K. Schlechta (Munich: 1954–56), III, p. 844.—TRANS.

ELEVEN

1. Plato, *Theaetetus*, 199b.—TRANS.
2. Cf. Husserl, I, pp. 80–81. [*Logical Investigations*, I, pp. 111ff. These quotations are in English both in Ortega's text and in Husserl's. They derive from John Stuart Mill, *An Examination of Sir William Hamilton's Philosophy*, ch. 21.—TRANS.]
3. Theodor Lipps, "Die Aufgaben der Erkenntnistheorie," *Philos[ophische] Monatsh[efte]*, XVI (1880), pp. 530f.
4. This interpolation is by the editor.—TRANS.
5. This interpolation is by the editor.—TRANS.
6. Ortega may be referring to Husserl, *Logical Investigations*. —TRANS.

TWELVE

1. John 18:38.—Trans.
2. Cf.Immanuel Kant, *Critique of Pure Reason*, trans. N. K. Smith, A 293/ B 350.—Trans.
3. Cf. Ortega, "To the Reader," in *Meditations on Quixote.*—Trans.
4. I have been unable to identify the original of this quote, which has therefore been translated directly from Ortega's Spanish version.—Trans.
5. Cf. Husserl, *Ideas*, I, § 104.—Trans.
6. Cf. Bernard Bolzano, *Theory of Science.*—Trans.
7. This interpolation is by the editor. Cf. Cervantes, *Don Quixote*, Part I, ch. 25.—Trans.
8. This interpolation is by the editor.—Trans.

FIFTEEN

1. Panini actually lived in the fourth century B.C.—Trans.
2. The expression actually used in this passage, *Queritur equidem* [He certainly complains], does not make sense in the context.—Trans.
3. Accordingly, this course was to be followed by another related to it, an event which apparently never took place.—Ed.
4. This interpolation is by the editor.—Trans.
5. Possibly the German philosopher Friedrich Jodl.—Trans.
6. In what follows, cf. Husserl, *Logical Investigations*, I, pp. 269ff. —Trans.
7. Instead of "smoke" (*el humo*), the passage reads "the human being" (*el humano*), which does not make sense in the context, either grammatically or in terms of the thrust of the whole passage. The reading "smoke" fits Ortega's analysis, and is confirmed—immediately and two paragraphs farther down— by the fact that he connects our seeing of smoke and our hearing of the word addressed to us with the intimations of fire and the other's thought, respectively.—Trans.
8. I have been unable to identify this reference.—Trans.
9. The manuscript ends at this point.—Ed.

1: ABSTRACTION

1. E. Husserl, *Logische Untersuchungen*, II. [*Logical Investigations*, I, pp. 353–54.—Trans.]
2. *Essay*, Books IV and II. [John Locke, *An Essay concerning Human Understanding*; the question mark was inserted by Ortega.—Trans.]
3. Cf. "Abstract."—Trans.
4. J. S.Mill, *An Examination of Sir William Hamilton's Philosophy*. [The passage is from the third edition, ch. 17. The emphasis is Ortega's.—Trans.]

2: ABSTRACT

1. No such entry is available.—Trans.
2. Cf. Aristotle, *Metaphysics*, 1028a.—Trans.
3. Ortega is apparently referring here to Aristotle's *Nicomachean Ethics*, 1142a.—Trans.
4. Cf. Aristotle, *Posterior Analytics*, 87a.—Trans.
5. John Stuart Mill, *A System of Logic*, Book I, chapter II, § 4.
6. [Christian] Wolff, [*Philosophia rationalis sive logica*], § 110.
7. [Wilhelm] Wundt, *Logik*, I, p. 106. [Since I have been unable to locate this work, the passage has been translated directly from Ortega's Spanish version.—Trans.]
8. [Alois] Höfler, *Grundlehren der Logik und Psychologie*, pp. 15–16. [The last interpolation in brackets in the text just quoted is by Ortega. Since I have been unable to locate this work, the passage has been translated directly from Ortega's Spanish version.—Trans.]
9. Ortega is referring specifically to Husserl's third "logical investigation."—Trans.

3: APPERCEPTION

1. Instead of *parte de él*, which I have translated as "part of the ego," the text reads *para de él*, which does not make sense. —Trans.

2. Cf. G. W. Leibniz, preface to *New Essays concerning Human Understanding*.—TRANS.

3. *Nouveaux essais* [*sur l'entendement humain* (*New Essays concerning Human Understanding*)], Book II, chapter 9, § 4.

4. G. W. Leibniz, *The Principles of Nature and Grace, Based on Reason*, included in part in his *Philosophical Papers and Letters*, ed. and trans. L. E. Loemker, 2nd ed., p. 637. A moment before, Leibniz had defined "perception" as "the inner state of the monad representing external things."—TRANS.

5. Kant, *Critique of Pure Reason*, A 99–100 and A 105–6.—TRANS.

6. Ibid., A 100–102 and A 118.—TRANS.

7. Ibid., A 103ff.—TRANS.

8. Ibid., B 131.—TRANS.

9. No such entry is available.—TRANS.

10. No such entry is available.—TRANS.

11. [Wilhelm] Wundt, *Grundriss der Psychologie*, [1896], chapter 2, §§ 8 and 9. [Since I have been unable to locate this work, the passages have been translated directly from Ortega's Spanish version.—TRANS.]

12. No such entry is available.—TRANS.

13. No such entry is available.—TRANS.

14. No such entry is available.—TRANS.

15. I have been unable to identify this author.—TRANS.

16. I have been unable to identify this author.—TRANS.

17. I have been able to identify neither the author nor the work Ortega refers to here.—TRANS.

18. Here the manuscript comes to an end.—ED.